I0485104

HELP! I NEED A JOB

Help! I Need A Job

The Desktop Guide to the Perfect Interview

Katreena K. Hayes-Wood

Writer's Showcase

San Jose New York Lincoln Shanghai

Help! I Need A Job
The Desktop Guide to the Perfect Interview

All Rights Reserved © 2002 by Katreena K. Hayes-Wood

No part of this book may be reproduced or transmitted in any form or by any means, graphic, electronic, or mechanical, including photocopying, recording, taping, or by any information storage retrieval system, without the permission in writing from the publisher.

Writer's Showcase
an imprint of iUniverse, Inc.

For information address:
iUniverse, Inc.
5220 S. 16th St., Suite 200
Lincoln, NE 68512
www.iuniverse.com

ISBN: 0-595-22075-4

Printed in the United States of America

Contents

Preface   vii

INTRODUCTION   1

PREPARATION   3

CHAPTER 1:   THE PREPARATION EQUATION   5

CHAPTER 2:   HOW TO GET A JOB INTERVIEW   19

CHAPTER 3:   LEARN TO NETWORK YOUR CONTACTS   25

CHAPTER 4:   MAKE A GREAT FIRST IMPRESSION   31

CHAPTER 5:   YOUR SKILLS, ACCOMPLISHMENTS, AND SELF-
             ASSESSMENT   39

CHAPTER 6:   DOING YOUR RESEARCH   55

CHAPTER 7:   HOW TO WRITE A RESUME   61

CHAPTER 8:   HOW TO WRITE EFFECTIVE COVER LETTERS   81

PRACTICE   87

CHAPTER 9:   TRADITIONAL INTERVIEW Q & A   89

CHAPTER 10: BEHAVIORAL INTERVIEWING   105

CHAPTER 11: ILLEGAL INTERVIEW QUESTIONS   113

CHAPTER 12: QUESTIONS YOU SHOULD PLAN TO ASK THE
             EMPLOYER   117

CHAPTER 13: QUESTIONS ABOUT SALARY, COMPENSATION, AND
             OFFER NEGOTIATIONS   123

OBSERVATION   129

CHAPTER 14: CALMING YOUR FEARS   131

CHAPTER 15: THE INTERVIEW   137

CHAPTER 16: TIPS OF THE TRADE   143

EVALUATION   155

CHAPTER 17: EVALUATING YOUR PERFORMANCE   157

CHAPTER 18: FOLLOW-UP   161

CHAPTER 19: OTHER AFTER-THE-INTERVIEW THINGS TO DO   167

CHAPTER 20: OFFER AND SALARY NEGOTIATIONS   171

CHAPTER 21: EVALUATING AN OFFER   175

CHAPTER 22: HAVE I TOLD YOU TO PREPARE?   183

About the Author   187

APPENDIX: QUICK REFERENCE   189

References   197

Preface

Everyone has a passion. Mine is helping people with their careers.

I've spent most of my career helping people with theirs: helping people define their career goals, fix their resumes, practice for interviews and negotiate compensation packages and employment offers. I have loved every minute.

It all began in January 1985 when I walked into an employment agency by the name of ESP (Extra Special People) Personnel. I hoped to find a job in public relations or journalism (my educational background). During the interview, the interviewer said to me, "We have an opening with our company and I think you'd be great in this business."

I said (because I really needed a job and thought I'd just keep on looking), "Sure, I'm interested."

It was on that day that I met Ann Freedle, the owner of ESP Personnel and the person I have to thank for introducing me and mentoring me in this wonderful business. Ann immediately took me under her wing and showed me the ropes. The one thing she taught me, that I use every day is to "Trust your instincts, because they will almost never fail you."

Several years later, my friend Dr. Barbara Roe-Snow encouraged me to begin teaching workshops on career development for adults. My instincts told me to go for it and I did. I started slow. I soon realized that I was good at speaking to groups and actually quite comfortable delivering career development material. It didn't take me long to realize that if I was going to deliver these great seminars that people would want something more than a four page handout to take home after the workshop. Thus began the creation of my first career development book: *Help! I Need a Job.*

Over the years, I have developed many processes that help make successful career planning easier. In this book, you will find several concepts that are specifically mine, frequently refined from something I learned from someone else. There are many people in the employment services industry and many of them are exemplary professionals. I have had the opportunity of working with a number of them.

As I mentioned, I am passionate about interviewing. However I am even more passionate about people loving what they do. The sad fact is that 86 percent of Americans are unhappy with their work. Research suggests that 50 to 80 percent of American workers are in the wrong jobs.

I realize that this book on interviewing won't change the world, but it might change yours. I believe that if you follow the principles in this book that you will interview with much more success.

Throughout history, we find that those people who have been the most successful have been good strategists. I also believe that to achieve true success we must plan for success. Seventy-five percent of this book is dedicated to planning, preparing, and practicing for a successful interview.

You will find four sections in my book: Preparation, Practice, Observation, and Evaluation. The first two sections, Prepare and Practice, are of prime importance! Everything you do before the interview pays dividends for every other aspect of what happens later in the interviewing process.

I have included samples and diagrams as often as possible to further explain the concepts I've presented. Many of them are also listed in the Appendix and Additional Resources sections in the back. In addition, I have placed all of the forms in this book on my website so you may print them out easily.

I have also included for quick reference Quix Fix and Quix Chex. Quix Fix is "what not to do" during an interview and Quix Chex is an interviewing checklist to ensure you have everything you need when you head off to an interview.

If you really do have an interview tomorrow, go to Quix Chex. This chapter condenses the highlights of this book.

However, if you want to guarantee interviewing success, I urge you to read the book from cover to cover. I can assure you this, it will help you improve your interviewing skills and get the job you want. Written for easy reading and understanding, my book offers concepts that you can use today for success tomorrow.

I hope you find *Help! I Need a Job* easy to read and understand, and helpful. If I can leave you with one thought before you begin, it should be this: Take the time to invest in yourself and your understanding of what is important to you in a career. If you take the time to discover these things, you will have more career success and can join the ranks of the 14 percent of Americans who love what they do!

Best wishes,
Katreena Hayes-Wood

Acknowledgements

Special thanks to:

Jeff Wood, my husband and life partner. Thank you for lighting the way, believing in me, and for making life's joyful journey sweeter.

Kalab, Keaton, Andrea and Seth, my children, for reminding me that love is life's reward.

Kleo Goforth and *Stan Hayes*, my parents. Thank you for giving me the foundation on which to build a wonderful life.

Grace W. Hayes, my grandma for teaching me about unconditional love.

Terez Sanguine, for her friendship and professional guidance.

Ann Freedle, for believing in me, giving me a chance, and then mentoring me.

Paul Ellis, winner of the "help–me–name–the–book," contest, my business associate and friend. Thanks for your support!

To all the others who have helped along the way—you know who you are. Thank you!

Thank you, all of you!
Katreena

Introduction

There is more to finding a job than sailing through an interview. And there is more to interviewing than showing up in your Sunday best accompanied by a great attitude and rehearsed answers to all the "key" questions. There are hundreds of books written on how to find a job that proscribe how to answer specific interviewing questions, what to say, how to act, dress, move, smile and shake hands.

Don't get me wrong. These elements are all vitally important to successful interviewing. But there is much more to interviewing than the interview.

Preparation is the single most important element to finding a job and interviewing well. Understanding the job-hunting process and having a well-thought-out plan to finding your next job is paramount to your success. A successful interview depends more on what you do before you shake the interviewer's hand than on what you do after the handshake.

This book will walk you through the process of finding a job from beginning to end, and will focus on successful interviewing. We will begin with what happens before the interview and will answer your questions about how to find jobs, how to use your network of friends and acquaintances to help you find job openings, how to uncover important information about the companies and people with whom you will interview, and finally what you can do after the interview that will make a huge difference to your interviewing success. It's simply written, easy to follow and loaded with examples and aids to help you along the path to finding your next job.

I've found that there are two types of interviewees—those who are naturally good at interviewing and those who are not. The first type of interviewee is usually comfortable with interviewing, perhaps because they've had lots of practice or because they are naturally conversant. The second type of interviewee, who is probably you since you're holding this book, is the person who is uncomfortable and nervous interviewing, or maybe a little rusty interviewing because of a lack of practice.

In any case, the topic of interviewing stresses most people. In fact, about 95 percent are anxious about interviewing and finding a new job. So relax. You are among friends.

This book is perfect for those of you who are just entering the job market and are new to interviewing, a bit rusty with the interviewing process, or maybe just need a little refresher course. All of the forms in this book can be printed from my website **www.csn4jobs.com.** Visit my website for forms, additional interviewing information and quick tips about finding a job.

If you're nervous about finding that new job, it means you really care and that's a good thing. What you do with your nervousness and how you channel that energy can make a tremendous difference to your job-finding efforts. Finding a job is a process and interviewing well is a skill, both of which you can learn. This book is a tool to teach you (or refresh your memory) and help you learn how to be successful at finding a job.

So let's begin. Your next job may be only a book away...

Preparation

Before anything else, getting ready is the secret of success.

—Henry Ford

1

The Preparation Equation

Napoleon, they say, won his battles from his tent; he planned his campaigns the night before so his military forces could execute successfully in the fore. Napoleon's battlefield and the front line of job hunting and interviewing are much the same. The groundwork wins the battle that often settles the war.

Preparing your interviewing strategy successfully takes planning. Developing a plan that determines your course of action and maps your progress is a sure path to victory. Knowing where you want to go makes planning your strategy easier. Understanding what kind of job you want and identifying your top skills with confidence is the key to good strategizing when it comes to interviewing successfully.

Why prepare?

Planning is like mowing the lawn! Who wants to do it? Obviously, you know it needs to be done, you know it will make a difference, it will enhance the appearance of your home—but quite honestly, you're busy. You need more time, better tools, and let's face it, you also need the desire to get the lawn mowed.

Now let's take it to the next level. Let's assume your best friend (or better, your mother) is coming to visit. Now your motivation to mow has just changed. You have somebody to impress, and suddenly you have the time, finely tuned tools, and motivation to mow your lawn!

Interviewing is like this. Often we need the incentive to get started. Ask yourself, where does your motivation come from? Sometimes your desire comes from real need and sometimes it comes from knowing it will make the difference in doing something right or doing it wrong.

Preparation does not take practice; it takes time. Think back to a situation in your past when you chose not to prepare. Most people can relate to choosing to not study for a test. How did things turn out? Now, think of a time when you chose to prepare. Did things turn out better? I don't need to sell you on the advantages of preparing because you've all taken a test and passed and taken a test and done poorly. What you chose to do before the test determined how well you did.

To a large degree, the success of your interview depends on what you do before you interview. The more work you put into planning for your interview, the more likely you are to get work!

In this section, we will cover every aspect of the interview that comes up before you ever go to an interview. I will discuss several topics that will help you prepare effectively for a successful interview. They include:

1. Defining what an interview is

2. Learning the different types of interviews so you can anticipate a course of action

3. Determining how to dress appropriately and successfully for an interview to make a great impression

4. Anticipating critical questions during an interview and formulating appropriate responses

5. Writing cover letters and interview related correspondence

6. Developing an effective, results-oriented resume

7. Constructing appropriate thank you letters and notes

8. Building and working an inside and an outside network

9. Determining your career profile through your skills self-assessment

10. Discovering where and how to find valuable information about companies, jobs, and interviewers

11. Keeping an accurate and thorough record of your job search

12. Planning for success with tools that help you stay focused and organized during your job search

Let's begin with a simple definition.

What is an interview?

An interview is a communication between two (or more) people to determine job match. With that definition in mind, it is important to understand the job search process and what's expected of you during an interview. Before you begin the process of planning your job search, let's discuss the types of interviews.

Types of Interviews

Consider the different types of interviews you may encounter:

- Information-gathering interview
- Phone interview (often a prescreening interview)
- One-on-one, hiring interview
- Group interview
- Behavioral interview
- Stress interview
- Mealtime interview
- On-the-job interview

- Salary negotiation/offer interview

Information-gathering Interviews

An interview you may consider before you choose to market yourself to a particular company is the **information-gathering** interview. This interview allows you to gather information about a company before you submit a resume for employment consideration.

The information-gathering interview may be as simple as calling the human resources or public relations department and asking them to mail you current information about the company. You can also do Internet or library research to gather information. You may want to set an actual appointment with human resources or a hiring manager you know or with whom you have a networking connection.

Probably the best way to gather information about a company is to talk to the gatekeeper, the receptionist. The person responsible for answering the company switchboard usually knows a lot about the company. He or she often spends a good part of the day answering questions about different aspects of the company and is usually helpful.

If you make an appointment to talk personally to someone within the company, assure him or her that you will only take 10 to 15 minutes, then stick to it. Keep an eye on your wristwatch and when your 15 minutes are up, give a reminder that the time you asked for is up. If the meeting has been productive up to this point, you will probably be urged to stay longer. If not, you have kept your promise to only take 10 to 15 minutes. If in the future you need to follow up with, your respect for the value of time will be remembered.

During the in-person, information-gathering interview make sure you are prepared in advance with a list of constructive questions. Never forget to ask if there are current openings for which you are qualified and/or if anyone else within the industry could offer you additional information.

After an interview send a thank you note to the interviewer or anyone else at the company who helped you gather data.

Phone Interviews

Designed to screen out the less qualified candidates is the **Phone Interview.** When you receive this type of call it usually comes outside of normal business hours. If you are prepared, you will increase your chances to make it past the phone elimination screening call. A few tips to help you organize include:

1. Plan to take the call in a quiet place where you can eliminate background noise and concentrate without interruption.

2. Have your Contact Information Notebook by the phone, as well as any other information that you might need. (I will explain the Contact Information Notebook later).

3. Have a pencil and paper by the phone to make notes. Make sure you write down the name of the person who is calling. Ask for the correct spelling of the name. This serves two purposes: it will give you time to locate the interviewer's specific company information in your Contact Information Notebook (CIN) and gather your thoughts; it will ensure that you have the name spelled correctly when you send your thank you note.

4. Have a copy of your current resume by the phone.

5. Stand while you speak. Your voice will sound stronger and more confident.

Note: Avoid using a cell phone for your interview. If this is your only viable option make sure that your battery is well charged and that you are in a location where your conversation will not be disrupted. An additional note: please do not attempt to do an interview while driving! It may sound obvious, but if you must be in your vehicle, pull over to conduct your interview.

One-on-one Hiring Interviews

Perhaps the most common interview is the **One-on-one Hiring Interview**. This meeting pairs you with one person from the company. During your initial contact, the interviewer usually provides you with details about the position, and frequently salary will be discussed. Occasionally the company's benefit package may be outlined. Depending on the technique and experience level of the interviewer, many things are possible and you should expect the unexpected. As I mentioned, many interviewers do not receive sufficient training as to how to interview and may spend the majority of the meeting talking. In this instance you will need to pay careful attention and look for opportunities to sell yourself. You will need to find occasions to demonstrate your skills as they relate to the job for which you are applying.

If on the other hand you have an interviewer who is skilled in interviewing, and you are prepared, you're in luck. Fortunately, this type of interviewer knows which questions to ask as well as how to delve into your background, which allows you the opportunity to provide valuable information regarding your match for the job. If you are unprepared, this type of interview can be devastating. Interviewers are looking for the best candidate and unless they are desperate, their job is to eliminate less-than-perfect candidates. Once again, I want to stress that being prepared allows you to become a preferred candidate.

Group Interviews

Group interviews are by far the most stressful interviews. It feels like you against them. The purpose of the group interview is much the same as the one-to-one interview. The twist is you have to respond to several different people and their personalities. This is where paying attention pays off! Make sure you acknowledge and give eye contact to each group member who asks questions. Early in the interview, you will need to pinpoint the group leader. You can usually identify this person because he or she begins and controls the flow of the interview.

This is also the person who is most likely to make the ultimate decision whether or not to make you an offer.

After the interview, ask each member for a business card if they have not been offered. This will ensure that when you send thank you letters to each group member you spell the names and titles correctly. It will also give you additional names to add to your networking list. Something I find very helpful to do is to number the business cards in sequence from left to right based on where people were sitting during the interview. If you have an opportunity later to speak to anybody who was present, you are more likely to remember who they are. You may also want to make notes on the back of an individual's business card if there is something important you wish to remember.

Later you may want to contact one of the group members if there is one with whom you connected particularly well. He or she may be willing to provide you with valuable information that will benefit your job search.

Behavioral interviews

I have already indicated that you may find yourself in a **Behavioral interview** during any interview. Behavioral interviewing is a method of interviewing used by employers to evaluate a candidate's experiences and behaviors in order to determine their future potential for career success. Most of the questions will start something like: "Give me an example of..." or "Tell me about a time when..."

The benefit of behavioral interviewing—if prepared—is that you can effectively demonstrate current or future career capability. You should always try to answer your questions by citing a specific example. By providing positive examples, you paint a picture for the interviewer of the type of employee you are.

Stress interviews

Stress interviews are exactly that—stressful. Conducted supposedly to see how you handle pressure, the interview may also be an instance of an untrained interviewer on a power trip. Regardless, stress questions evaluate your emotional reflexes, creativity, or attitudes while under pressure. In my research for this book, I found that very few interviewers ask trick questions. Only about 12 percent pose them to look for hesitation from a job candidate before answering.

If the job for which you are applying has elements of stress in the duties, expect a stressful interview. Therefore be prepared for interviewer stares, long periods of silence, quick questions, interruptions to your answers, and use of job-related sarcasm. Since off-the-wall questions tend to jolt your equilibrium or put you in a defensive posture, the best way to handle them is to stay calm. When you realize you are in a stressful interviewing situation try, practicing these techniques:

- Calm down and take a deep breath.

- Answer as many questions or as much of a question as you can until the next interruption.

- Do not let silences fluster or unnerve you.

- Do not be defensive; keep your cool.

- Consider responses carefully and don't be afraid to think an answer through.

- If you don't know an answer, say so. Sometimes the interviewer is looking for someone who isn't afraid to say "I don't know the answer."

Of course, your sense of humor will come in handy at this time, provided you don't go overboard. You might try a light comment about having sweaty palms or a parched throat and that you are usually cool under extreme pressure. If you do become very unnerved, keep in mind that this is not the only job in the working world. Consider how stressful the position might be and whether you want that much stress in your life. Remember that usually the stress interview is associated with stressful jobs.

Mealtime Interviews

One very deceiving and stressful type of interview is the **Mealtime interview.** Talking to someone over food has a tendency to relax us and we may be more willing to share information—often too much information. You need to practice caution in these types of interviews.

Some company executives I know use this interviewing method to weed candidates out as early as possible, and some have ways of eliminating applicants in the final stages of the interviewing process. This is where being prepared can really pay off and advance you to the final selection category.

A client of mine uses the mealtime interview as a strategy to view several candidates together in a casual setting, but judges them on their professional demeanor. This also allows my client to see how job candidates perform under pressure through observing their actions during the meal. Some of the qualities my client watches for include: what they order, how they handle eating while answering questions, how they handle the pressure of the presence of competitors for the position, and whether they order alcohol or exhibit inappropriate or unprofessional behavior.

I have another client who will intentionally order an alcoholic beverage (or something that sounds alcoholic) to see if the candidate will also order alcohol. *Never order an alcoholic beverage during a luncheon or dinner interview.* The interviewer may intend to create a friendly, easy atmosphere in which you can be very comfortable. The interviewer may also choose to get bombed. In any case, you stay sober. When all is said and done if you end up spending an evening with a drunk, you may seriously consider if he or she represents the type of company you would enjoy working for. However, if the interviewer was simply trying to put you at ease, take that into consideration as well.

On-the-job interviews

One of the more interesting interviews is the **On-the-job interview**. This type of interview permits the interviewer to see how you actually perform on the job and is quite common for sales-related positions. The hiring manager will ask you to follow along for part of a day (or even an entire day) to show you what is involved with the job. If you are a top contender for a position, you can expect the possibility of this type of interview. What the interviewer is looking for in general is how assertive you are with people you don't already know, or the types of questions you ask after a vendor visit.

If you are applying for a position that is sales and service related, you may want to request this type of interview. You will have an opportunity to experience how well you get along with potential co-workers and vendors. This type of interview is also an excellent way to discover if "this is the job for you."

Negotiation/offer interviews

Finally, there is the **Negotiation/offer interview,** which I will cover in more depth in the next section. As you can imagine this can be the most stressful interview of all—stressful because you are getting an offer you most likely want, and knowing that your acceptance of the offer depends on the salary and compensation package. Relax! If you have proceeded this far, the company wants to hire you and they want to make you a fair offer. If you have determined they are a good company to work for, you can expect them to make a reasonable offer. Anticipate an offer that works for both sides.

Now that you are armed with a general understanding of the different types of interviews you should anticipate, you're ready to look ahead to discover how to find the types of jobs you want. What do most people do to find their next job? My research shows that 97 percent of job hunters simply mail out resumes, post resumes on the web and wait to get results. Obviously this method works or fewer people would rely on this method. However, it is time consuming and unproductive when you look at how much time you spend to secure an average of 10 interviews for every 100 resumes mailed/faxed/emailed. If you want to capitalize your time and effort, there is a better and more efficient way to find a job. You'll need to be more proactive.

Know what type of interview to prepare for

Know what you're in for ahead of time. There are several types of interviews, and when you schedule your interview it is perfectly acceptable to ask what type to expect. For example, you may ask, "Is my interview going to be a group interview?" It helps to know what is going to happen so that you are better able to prepare.

A good friend of mine was getting ready to fly to northern California's Silicon Valley for a very important job interview with a high-tech firm. She had done her homework. She knew everything she possibly could know about the company she was visiting. She had even done a little digging and found out information about the hiring manager who had scheduled her interview. The problem was she never interviewed with that particular person. She arrived and was met by a Human Resources representative who took her to a conference room filled with 13 people (needless to say 13 was a very unlucky number for her that day) and the interview was a disaster. She was totally, unprepared. She never thought to ask what type of interview to expect and therefore had a horrible surprise.

Don't ever get caught by surprise this way! Ask! Ask! Ask! If you don't get an answer as to what type of interview you should expect, ask again until you do get an answer that will allow you to sleep the night before. *I don't need to preach to you about the benefits of a good night's sleep, especially before an important meeting.*

Not all hiring managers are prepared to interview you. Often they don't get training on how to interview and may not always ask the right questions. It is during an interview like this that it is up to you to make sure your answers focus on your skills and accomplishments as they relate to the job opening for which you are interviewing. Pay attention to the interviewer's style. Is it formal or informal, does the interviewer ask questions or give details about the position? Or, do they spend most of the time discussing the job opening?

Where are the jobs?

Finding jobs is easy if you know where to look. Many of you already have a good idea of where to search for opportunities. Some of the resources to monitor for job openings include:

1. The Internet

2. The classified section of your local newspaper

3. Your personal and professional network of friends, business colleagues and professional associations

Later, I will discuss in detail how to use those sources to your best advantage. Right now let's talk about what's really bothering you (and what bothers almost everyone, for that matter).

The problem most people have is what to do **after** they find a job that interests them.

As I mentioned, 97 percent of job seekers send out resumes. The fact is that for every 100 resumes sent out, you can expect an average of 20 telephone-screening calls. Of those 20 calls, about 10 will result in job interviews. From those 10 interviews, you will most likely get one job offer. As you can see, the odds are low.

If you want the odds to increase in your favor, you'll have to be more proactive. Have you ever wondered what would happen if you picked up the phone and called the company—or better, personally taken your resume to the company and asked to speak to the person doing the hiring?

Yes, you probably wondered what would happen, but you've probably never acted on that thought. Act on it! See what happens. It'll surprise you. If you're willing to make the effort and do the work of calling or visiting companies, your chances of getting the job you want will increase exponentially.

Recruiters and hiring managers are bombarded daily with resumes they don't want or can't use. When they have openings, their job is to eliminate candidates' resumes. If your resume isn't perfectly suited for the job, you're eliminated before you ever have a chance to make your case. You can see why sending a resume seems like a waste of time. However, the majority of employers I spoke with in doing the research for this book told me they returned calls and spoke with people who called about specific job openings. Most hiring managers said candidates who did the work to get through to them impressed them.

If you're not sure whether you should send your resume or not, use the following rule. It will save you time and effort. Your credentials should match at least 75 percent of those listed in the job description or classified ad; if they don't, don't bother sending your resume. There will always be someone who possesses at least 75 percent of the listed qualifications. Don't send your resume unless you're one of them.

2
How to Get a Job Interview

Be proactive! Let me define a few simple techniques that will make a tremendous difference in your success rate for getting interviews for the jobs you want.

Getting an interview can be tough stuff if you're not sure which approach to take. Below I've outlined four very different strategies. You will discover that each works wonders opening doors to the companies for which you are most interested. These methods include:

Cold Calling
Alert the Competition
Working Your Networking
Pre-interview Confirmation Note*

*Important Tip: Once you have secured an interview you need to send the person with whom you will interview a confirmation note. Almost no one does this, but I guarantee you the interviewer will remember! Sending the **pre-interview confirmation note** is almost as important as sending a thank you note after your interview.*

The **Cold Calling** method is perhaps the most difficult and challenging of all four strategies for obtaining interviews. Cold Calling is simply that—making a call cold. The interesting thing is that cold calls make every other call related to it a warm call. Warm calls open doors. Cold calls allow you to knock.

When you cold call, you're calling on a person at a company, either by phone or in person, who you do not know. A cold call doesn't mean you don't have any information or a strategy planned. To make a successful cold call, try this procedure:

When calling by telephone

Step 1. Call the company you wish to interview with and get the name of the person who is responsible for hiring people with your background.

Step 2. Get the name of the receptionist. Take notes on the back of your Company Contact Card (included in appendix). Notes might include: what the company does, number of employees, how long they have been in business, etc. (The receptionist will be happy to answer these types of questions for you).

Step 3. Wait until later in the day, or perhaps as late as the next day. When you call back, ask for the person named by the receptionist. When that person answers the phone, begin your dialogue with: "Mr./Ms. Contact Name, my name is Katreena. I spoke with your receptionist Sally Jones earlier today and she indicated that you're the person in charge of hiring marketing personnel." (Pause long enough for them to acknowledge that they are in fact that person).
Continue with: "I noticed that you had an ad* for an opening in the marketing department for which I am very qualified. I was hoping that I could come by some time during the next couple of days for a short visit and drop off a resume, and take ten minutes to talk with you about the opening." (Again, pause to await their response).
Continue: "Actually, I'll be in your area next Monday, and then again on Wednesday. Which of those days works better for you?" You may also want to give them a choice of morning or after-

noon. (Note: giving the hiring manager a choice offers you a much better chance for success).

Step 4. After you have confirmed a date for your interview, send a follow up note confirming the details of the meeting. If the meeting is the next day, get their email address if possible, and send a confirmation that way.

*Note: In the event that the company does not have a posted job opening, you may start your dialogue with something like: "I am interested in talking to you about the success of your _____ department." Don't mention that you'll bring a resume. This call should not sound like a solicitation but more information gathering in nature.

When calling in person

Step 1. Visit the company you wish to interview with and obtain a business card from the receptionist for the person who is responsible for hiring people with your background.

Step 2. Get the name of the receptionist and write it on the business card. Make any other notes on the back of the card. Notes might include: what the company does, number of employees, how long they have been in business, etc. (The receptionist will be happy to answer these types of questions for you).

Note: It they offer you an application, do not sit there to fill it out. Appear to be busy, not desperate. Never leave your resume with the receptionist on a cold call.

Step 3. Wait until later in the day, or perhaps as late as the next day but no longer, to call back. When you call back, ask for the person named by the receptionist. When that person answers the phone, begin your dialogue with: "Mr./Ms. Contact Name, my name is Katreena. I spoke with your receptionist Sally Jones earlier today and she indicated that you're the person in charge of hiring marketing personnel." (Pause long enough for them to acknowledge that they are in fact that person).

Continue with: "I noticed that you had an ad* for an opening in the marketing department for which I am very qualified. I was hoping that I could come by for a short visit over the course of the next couple of days and drop off a resume and take ten minutes to talk with you about the opening." (Again, pause to await their response).

Continue: "Actually, I'll be in your neighborhood on Monday, and then again on Wednesday. Which of those days works better for you?" You may also want to give them a choice of morning or afternoon. (Note: giving the hiring manager a choice offers you a much better option for success).

Step 4. After you have confirmed a date for your interview, send a follow up note confirming the details of the meeting. If the meeting is the next day, get their email address if possible and send a confirmation that way.

*Note: In the event that the company does not have a posted job opening, you may start your dialogue with something like: "I am interested in talking to you about the success of your _____ department." Don't mention that you'll bring a resume. This call should not sound like a solicitation but more information gathering in nature.

As you can see, there isn't too much difference between the phone and in-person encounter except how much time you spend engaged in each activity. However, if you are able to get in to see the hiring manager on your first cold call visit, make certain you are prepared. When you tell them you only want ten minutes of their time, stick to that time frame. When you reach the allotted time limit let them know you've taken up the time you asked for. If they are interested, they'll ask you to stay. If you're prepared, they are also likely to ask you to stay.

Alert the Competition is a sharp technique. Simply stated, this approach to obtaining an interview is clever and usually works. The goal of this strategy is to create a sense of urgency with the hiring manager at the company you want to join. Here's how it works:

Contact the hiring managers of a company in an industry for which you are interested in working (using the cold calling method) until you find one willing to meet with you.

Next contact six other companies that are competitors of company number one.

Let the other six hiring managers know that you are talking to company number one about a potential offer, but before you accept an offer, you want a chance to meet with them first. The upshot here is you will usually get one or two of the six competitors to consider you for interviews and/or offers of employment.

A note of caution here is that you create a sense of urgency but it won't last long. You need to act quickly and have your strategy planned out in advance.

Finally, **Networking** is probably your most powerful and effective tool in job-hunting. Literally every person you know should be part of your network. Most of us are acquainted with 200 to 300 people apiece. With these numbers in mind, it could be assumed that a job offer is probably only a few calls away.

In the next chapter, I delve into the essential tool of networking. Learning to build and work your network will be invaluable to your job search and interviewing success.

3

Learn to Network Your Contacts

Networking is a powerful tool. **KNOW YOUR NETWORK.**

We have all heard the famous cliché: It is not what you know, but who. We have all heard a story about someone who got a great break because they had a great connection. If you don't already have those "special" connections, you'll need to make your own.

I have a good friend who was having a particularly difficult task finding a job; in fact, she had been looking for a job for almost a year. She had followed the standard routine of sending resumes and following up but just wasn't making any headway in her job search. She has an impressive employment history and great experience, so it seemed the market for her specific skills was flat. During this time she was teaching a class at her church and one of her fellow teachers told her that her husband's company was looking for someone to work with local schools and their insurance coverage plans (an occupation that perfectly suited my friend).

Without ever running an ad or calling an employment agency the company found the perfect candidate for their job and my friend found the perfect career she'd been hoping for. To this day they've never seen her resume. They didn't need to because she had an inside connection.

Most of us don't realize how many people we really know until we begin to make a list. Have any of you ever planned a wedding? You start with a simple list of 40 to 50 people and before you know it, you

have 150 names written down. You can easily take that list of 150 people and think of another 150 people who know the first 150 people.
See how it works? Building a list from which to network just takes a little time with pen to paper (or fingers to keyboard).

I'd like to begin by defining the different types of networks.

Who is your *inside network*? To build an inside network, your
goal should be to find someone within the company in which you are
interested in interviewing with whom to network. If you do not know
of anyone, use your outside network to find an inside contact, if possible. When that doesn't work, use the company's gatekeeper, the receptionist.

Often the receptionist is happy to share information about the company, including website address, hiring manager's names and if you are
very lucky, personal information about the person with whom you may
interview. This person can be a key inside network contact. Never
overlook the power of a gatekeeper; always treat them with respect and
courtesy! Sometimes you will encounter a less-than-helpful receptionist; the lack of enthusiasm is often because they get numerous calls
from people trying to mine information about company employees
and are under strict orders about not giving out too much information.

Don't let this discourage you. Try calling before or after hours. If
you're lucky you might get the relief receptionist who may not be so
well trained and may more readily share information.

With any networking contact, you may want to consider the following questions:

- For this job, what skills or training do you require?

- Are there skills or special qualities that help entry-level job seekers?

- What advice would you give to someone interested in your company?

- How do you see my skills fitting into your company?

- Do you know if your company prefers doing an inside hire for this position?

- Is there someone you would recommend I talk to that could give me additional information that would benefit me?

Who is your *outside network*? Your outside network is anyone you know. Remember the wedding list? Well, that's a good place to start. If you've never planned a wedding, pretend you are planning one now. (Who knows? Maybe you can use it later when you do need to plan a real wedding.)

Anyway, back to your network. Most of the people you know work, right? These people have friends who work, too. Through associations, you can quickly build an extensive network. As a matter-of-fact, any contact you have that might be able to help you secure an interview, provide information about open positions at companies, or knows someone who may have information is part of your network infrastructure.

There are several ways to begin your list of networking contacts:

- Look at your former jobs. Who do you know with whom you worked well who might know someone who has an opening or a lead?

- Look at your friends, acquaintances, and yes—even family. Who do they know who may be able to help?

- Look at your professional associations and other non-profit organizations you belong to: churches, children's schools, daycare centers, professional and trade associations, volunteer organizations. All can be excellent sources for networking leads and potential job interviews.

A tool I often recommend that candidates use to expand their network is the **business card resume.** It's simply a business card on one side with contact information and job-related strengths, experience etc. on the reverse side. An example follows:

Front Side   Reverse Side

| **Andrea C. Wood**
1234 West Happy Street
Anytown, State 12345

Home Phone: 123-456-7890
Office Phone: 234-567-8910
Cell Phone: 345-678-9102

Email Address: acwood@email.com | **Objective:** To obtain a position that allows me to use my strong organization skills in a productive environ-ment that offers advancement opportunities
Skills:
• Proficient w/ MS Windows, Lotus 123, Peachtree
• Excellent verbal and written commnication skills
• Successfullly managed and directed 10 office personnel

Awarded *Employee of the Year, 1998, 2000* |

The business card resume is easy to carry and is easier to pass out to networking contacts and potential employers.

Keeping track of your network

Next, you will want to use a tracking form to document the progress of the contacts you make. Below is a form you may consider using; it is also available on my website at: **www.csn4jobs.com.** You may want to use a three-ring binder, or **Contact Information Notebook**, with alphabetized dividers to keep your list well organized.

Keep your job search book by the telephone. When an employer or a network contact calls, you should have your Contact Information Notebook close-at-hand to access and provide information to the caller.

You may want to use the Notes/Comments area to paste classified want ads, or information to refer to later. If the information doesn't fit on the front, use the back of the page. Make sure you alphabetize by the company name so information is easy to find.

Note: Remember to keep your Contact Information Notebook by your telephone!

Work your network

Finally, don't be afraid to work your network. Pick up the phone and call the people you know who might be able to help. You'd want to help them if they called you. So, do it. Pick up the phone.

More than a decade ago when I was the single mother of two pre-schoolers, I was laid off unexpectedly. I was devastated and tremendously stressed. I called a very good friend of mine, also a single mother and an executive recruiter, and asked for her help. She referred me to a private college looking for someone in their Career Services department. I immediately contacted the school and within a week had an offer. Don't be afraid to work your personal network.

When you make your calls, let the person with whom you are networking know that you are in the job market. Ask if they know of anyone or any company with an opening in your industry or area of expertise. Ask them if you can send a resume or if they'd keep you in mind if they hear of career opportunities for which you are qualified.

After you begin working your network, stay organized. Keep notes in your Contact Information Notebook, send thank you notes to anyone who offers any kind of advice, contact, or help. People remember thank you notes. You probably remember the last thank you note you received; that's because people don't send them much anymore. Send them; politeness pays off.

Contact Information Form

Contact Name: _____

Telephone Number: _____   Fax Number: _____

Email Address: _____

Information and Notes:

Date	Why Contacted	Comments	Special Notes	Follow-Up Date

4
Make a Great First Impression

First impressions count! First impressions will make or break you! It's time to look at the image you project to those with whom you come in contact. What is their first impression of you? You've spent a considerable amount of time focusing on the topics relating to external matters. Now you need to spend an equal amount of time focusing on yourself.

Dating and interviewing are quite similar!

I'm sure many of you have been on blind dates and can relate to the awful feeling of seeing someone walk through the door and hoping that they're not the person you're supposed to be meeting. When they walk through the door and look like the answer to prayer, the relief is almost overwhelming.

Professional Image

Do not under estimate the power of the first 20 seconds of your interview! Most people decide within that span of time whether or not they like you. For a moment, think about what goes through your mind when you first meet someone. What's the first thing that happens? Do you decide if you like the way they look, or how they talk? What about an accent in their voice, or clothes that are oddly matched or drastically out of style—do you notice these things? If you notice, just imagine how an interviewer is trained to size up a person that may represent his or her company.

With only 20 seconds in which to make a good first impression, be sure you plan ahead. You should know what to expect before you arrive at an interview. However, there are some general pointers you may find helpful during the **Halo Effect Period**—that 20 second period of time when an employer decides if they like you and would consider you a top candidate to work for their company.

The best advice for the first 20 seconds of your interview is to:

• Smile

• Make appropriate eye contact

• Offer a firm handshake

This next bit of advice will sound like your mother, but here goes…stand tall, shoulders back and relax your face. Let your confidence shine through. Make sure that you are dressed professionally for the interview. Please be well groomed and mannered.

If you get an A for this assignment you will have a strong chance at a second interview.

Are you ready?

You've done your homework. You've built a strong network, obtained solid information about companies and the job market; you even have a few companies that want to interview you. So, what's next? How can you further prepare yourself for making a positive impact on your interviewing campaign?

Looking professional at an interview is perhaps the single most important thing that can make a difference. As I mentioned earlier, we have all made a judgment about someone before we can stop ourselves. Hiring managers do the same thing, but for a very good reason. They must hire the most qualified applicant for the job. Usually they have learned that an applicant who takes time and care with his or her appearance will take time and care with the job. They believe that sloppy dressers make sloppy employees.

Do not be a sloppy dresser. There is no excuse for it.

If you cannot afford to buy a new suit, try a second-hand consignment store. Many have very nice, brand name professional attire at affordable prices. There are even organizations that will help you find interviewing clothing at no cost through the referral of an agency. You may also wish to check with local churches. They often have resources to help with clothing. There are also thrift and resale stores like Goodwill, The Salvation Army, Deseret Industries, and Savers.

There are some basic rules to professional dress. The quick version is: **dark on bottom, light on top.** Pants, skirts, shoes, socks, and stockings should be in dark shades and shirts and blouses should be in light tones. Choose colors that are conservative and compliment your coloring. I have found that most people seem to instinctively select colors that look good on them. Some basic rules to adhere to include:

- Avoid casual looks

- Avoid loud and overly trendy accessories

- Your image equals your credibility

- Better to overdress than under-dress

- Avoid wearing perfume and cologne

- Dress for the job you want

- Dress for the season, but still be business-like

- Avoid trendy colors

- If in doubt, do not wear it

- Keep your outfit simple

Professional Dress Dos and Don'ts

If you are in doubt about what looks great on you and defines the professional style you desire, these simple rules should help you:

Women:

- Wear a suit, skirt and tailored jacket in a conservative style. Make sure your outfit is freshly laundered and pressed.

- Dresses should have sleeves with simple and conservative lines. Avoid anything sleeveless, unless it is under a jacket.

- Avoid very short skirts. Skirts should be no higher than 4" above the center of the knee.

- Be feminine, but business-like.

- Makeup should be conservative.

- Hair should be in a conservative style, and pulled back if long.

- Nails should be short to medium length with light to clear polish.

- Shoes should be the color of your skirt or pants—never lighter. Absolutely no colored shoes with black hose!

- Socks or stockings should be the same color as your shoes, unless you wear tan stockings. Note: You may want to carry an extra pair of pantyhose in your car for emergencies.

- Use a purse or briefcase that matches your outfit, preferably your shoes. Hold your handbag in your left hand so your right hand is free for a handshake.

Men:

- Wear a suit, preferably in a dark color. Blue and grays work well. Make sure outfit is clean and pressed.

- Select solid colored shirts with conservative ties.

- Blazers and slacks are allowable, with a shirt and tie. Remember to dress for the job you want.

- Keep accessories to a minimum. Eliminate earrings or flashy jewelry.

- Wear hair in a conservative style. Facial hair can be a turn-off.

- Never wear white athletic socks with slacks. Make sure socks are the same color, or with a coordinating print, as your pants.

- Wear dark-colored shoes.

- As listed above for women, take a briefcase or portfolio. Make sure to carry it in your left hand so your right hand is free for a handshake.

It pays to look professional. Studies show applicants that dress more professionally get more and better job offers. As a matter-of-fact, more than 62 percent of the hiring managers I spoke to claim they give greater consideration to applicants who dress professionally, even if the job doesn't require professional dress. It stands to reason then that a little planning and perhaps spending up front will pay big dividends later. As I've stated repeatedly, follow the simplified approach: dress dark on bottom and light on top, keep your outfit simple and conservative. Remember the most effective accessories still are a great smile, and a firm handshake complemented with confident eye contact. Take that formula for success and throw in a strong dose of enthusiasm and you're good to go!

The Basic Career Wardrobe

Many of you may not be in a position to go out a purchase a new wardrobe for interviewing. However if you carefully select and coordinate a few basic garments you may be able to purchase a few new items and make a very big difference. Choose solid colors that you can mix and match or multi-colored accessories.

Women:

- Two three-piece suits (jacket, skirt, pants). For summer, a light colored suit, with a darker outfit for winter

- One solid color blazer

- One sweater (cardigan)

- Two basic skirts (straight or flared) to compliment your figure, knee length (no higher than 4" above) or longer

- One classic pair of pants

- One pinstripe blouse

- Two solid color blouses

- Two shirts

- One shirtdress (to wear with the blazer)

- One classic dress, with several accessories to change the look

- One all-weather coat

- Shoes (light tan for summer, black for winter, pumps no more than 2" high)

- Accessories (scarves, jewelry, belts, etc.). Keep styles simple and elegant

Men:

- Suits should be as year-around as possible. Wool selections are available that can be worn during all four seasons.

- Jackets or blazers are more versatile if they are solid in color or have a subdued pattern.

- Pants should offer a variety of medium to dark colors and durable fabrics.

- Shirts should include a variety of whites, other lights, and stripes. You could include fashionable offerings in chambray or denim, depending on the image you need to project and your personal preferences.

- Ties of medium width are classic and can be worn with current fashions.

- Belts should be made of good quality leather in a subdued color that will coordinate with pants.

- Choose shoes that lace up for a more formal professional look and wear slip-on shoes for casual professional wear.

- Socks should blend with your slacks and shoes and should come up over your calves. Absolutely no athletic socks with dress slacks! When you sit, your pant leg hem should not hike up higher than mid-calf.

- Coats also should offer classic details in good quality fabric. Full tailored and all-weather versions are acceptable.

5
Your Skills, Accomplishments, and Self-assessment

What are your most marketable skills? This chapter will help you define your career profile, specific job interests, and career direction. If you already know what area you are most interested in, what job you want, or the direction your career needs to go, you may want to skip this chapter.

On the other hand, if you want to delve into your natural skills, abilities, industry interests and environmental preferences to see just where you would be most professionally successful, set aside some time and do the self-assessments. This chapter will help you answer the really tough question: "What do I want to be when I grow up?"

What do you really want in a career? Some of you will already know the answer to this question. Unfortunately, 86 percent of American workers are unhappy with their career choices. In planning for career success, it helps to know what you love to do.

Note: You may even want to consider having a full-blown career assessment done. I provide just such an assessment through STRIVE for Students, a sister-company. STRIVE offers an assessment that based on an individual's behavior, interests, attitudes, and values can predict jobs and industries in which he or she will excel. For more information on this assessment, contact me directly at 623-561-6838.

In one of the my workshops "How to Re-engineer your Career"™ I spend a considerable amount of time assessing the personality, natural strengths and talents, learning style, interests, and environmental preferences of the attendees. It is my belief that the more people know about what's important to them, what they enjoy, what they are passionate about, and what makes them tick, the better able they are to focus and plan for successful careers and lives.

Defining your skills

Let's begin by defining skills.

A skill is an ability, talent, knowledge, or personal quality that results in effective performance. There are five categories of skills, all of which you possess. You may want to take out a pencil and paper and jot down the skills you have in each category

There are five categories of skills:

1. **General skills**—think of these skills as generic in nature.

2. **Specific skills**—these are the skills that you have "specifically" learned to use such as using a particular piece of equipment or a certain type of software.

3. **Transferable skills**—these skills are fundamental to the specific industry or career you have chosen. You can take these skills with you to any new job.

4. **Interpersonal skills**—these are your people skills; think of this category in terms of how you get along with and interact with others.

5. **Special skills**—these are the special skills that make you unique. They are your basic and most natural talents and abilities: like attention to detail, putting things together, or leading people or projects.

Skills are nothing more than your accomplishments translated into deeds. Think about the things you have done—those things of which you are most proud—as skills. Without certain skills you would not be able to accomplish certain deeds.

Accomplishments are skills translated into deeds.

Unfortunately, we often have a tendency to overlook our best skills and accomplishments because we sometimes don't recognize them for what they are. Identifying your skills may be difficult if you tend to...

• think in terms of skills as being **tasks.**

• take your natural skills and abilities for **granted.**

• **forget** about past skills that you have used.

• be too **modest** about your talents and what you do well.

Now, take a look at your specific skill set. You will begin by taking a comprehensive skills evaluation. As you work your way through the assessment, you will detect an area (or areas) in which you seem to have more skills or interests than in others. This is actually what you want to have happen.

What you are looking for is something from which to work. I call it "CareerMapping"™. CareerMapping™ is an exercise that will allow you to define what type of work best suits you, and is a starting point for your resume, and a blueprint for your career success.

Compiling your accomplishments and discovering your skills

Take a few minutes and find examples in your work, education, or personal achievement history that you could use effectively during a job interview. Answer the following questions by citing examples from your work experience where you:

1. Reduced costs _____

2. Increased performance _____

3. Increased efficiency _____

4. Reduced time _____

5. Improved reliability _____

6. Provided better controls _____

7. Improved working conditions _____

Examples might include reducing costs on project materials, increased performance by team members by offering incentive programs, or improved reliability of quality controls. For each example you'll need to have a work/school/personal story to illustrate your accomplishment.

After identifying your accomplishments, you are ready to do your self-evaluation and discover your natural skills and abilities. Below is the self-evaluation. Some of you may already have a very clear picture of what type of work you are looking for and how your skills fit into that career type. If this is the case, you may want to skip over this chapter.

If you are not sure what you want to do or if you want to have a more thorough understanding of what skills you have, consider spending and hour or so and taking the time to work through the self-evaluation.

The Cheat Sheet

To help them evaluate their accomplishments, I share a few favorite tips with my candidates on what I call their **cheat sheet**—or skills list. This list is for the interview and needs to be concise and brief—something you can tuck away and pull out to review. It works best on a 3"x5" index card that fits into your pocket and on which you have written your important qualifications and special skills—the skills you will want to evaluate before and recall during your interview. Here's the information I recommend you list on your cheat sheet:

1. Your three greatest strengths

2. Your greatest weakness (think through how you have overcome your weakness and turned it into a positive lesson)

3. Something you have accomplished or done of which you are very proud

4. Maybe even your personal mission statement, a favorite quote, creed, or objective for the type of job you want

This little tool will do wonders while you wait. Pull it out of your pocket or portfolio and read it as you wait for your interview and you will find it gives you a little boost of confidence. If you get nervous during the interview when the interviewer asks questions about your strengths or weaknesses (and they usually will) visualize your pocket cheat sheet. It will help! You may even wish to take it out and refer to it during your interview.

Taking the skills self-assessment

You may want to begin by copying this page so you can use it again later if needed, or you may choose to visit my website **www.csn4jobs.com** where you can print the self-assessment pages.

ENVIROMENTAL PREFERENCE ASSESSMENT

In considering your ideal work environment, which of the selections below most appeal to you?

Sound & Noise Preference

- quiet
- noise, like cars or street noises
- music
- people talking

Physical Environment Preference

- sitting at a desk or table
- standing at a table or machinery
- moving or walking around
- no preference

Interaction with People Preference

- being by myself with the door closed

- being with other people who are quiet

- being with other people who are talking or doing things

- no preference

Type of Work Environment Preference

- office

- factory/warehouse

- store

- hospital (or similar)

- outdoors

Attire & Dress Preference

- casual

- uniform

- professional

- no preference

Work Hours and Shifts Preference

- day shift (typically 7am–5pm)

- swing/evening shift (typically 3pm–midnight)

- graveyard/night shift (typically midnight–7am)

Schedule Preference

- weekdays: (circle days that you prefer working)

    Monday Tuesday Wednesday Thursday Friday

- weekends: (circle days that you prefer working)

    Saturday Sunday

- no preference

NATURAL ABILITIES, SKILLS AND TALENTS ASSESSMENT

Skills Category:

Are you most comfortable with…(Choose one that most fits you)

☐ Gather Information   ☐ Connect with people   ☐ Work with things

Skills Inventory

From the list below, check all of the things you enjoy or do well:

Analytical

- discovering
- measuring
- working with numbers
- games like chess
- working with money
- doing experiments
- using calculators

Nurturing

- helping others
- listening
- getting along with others
- making friends
- baby-sitting
- leading teams of people
- understanding people

- doing puzzles
- organizing
- comparing things/numbers
- playing with numbers in my head

- group games or projects
- protecting
- teaching others
- nursing

Mechanical

- fixing things
- taking things apart
- inventing
- running machines
- taking care of cars
- handling tools
- building things
- shaping things
- lifting/moving things
- delivering things
- doing craft projects

Systematic

- working on computers
- reading or telling stories
- memorizing names or numbers
- budgeting money
- jigsaw puzzles
- following directions
- putting things in order
- writing neatly
- collecting information
- memory for details
- filing information

Enterprising

- leading or directing
- setting/meeting deadlines
- making decisions
- selling
- planning meetings/parties
- speaking in front of others
- taking risks

Creative

- thinking of new ideas
- photographing
- dancing to music
- cooking, planning meals
- coordinating colors
- designing
- making layouts/drafting

- talking easily with strangers
- planning action/activities
- coming up with new projects
- getting others involved
- using my imagination
- drawing or sketching
- planting a garden
- expressing emotion

Take a careful look at the skills inventory list and circle the top 10 skills that you most enjoy using:

1. _____

2. _____

3. _____

4. _____

5. _____

6. _____

7. _____

8. _____

9. _____

10. _____

Looking at the skills you have identified, determine what talents you are using in your current occupation. What skills fit into an industry or job that you would like to be involved in? Do you see more skills listed in an industry you would prefer to move into instead of the area in which you are currently working? If so, you need to take a closer look at those skills and potential business arenas.

After you have taken a closer look at the results of your self-evaluation and determined an industry or job that interests you and parallels your skills inventory you will want to begin researching the market-place.

Ask yourself which industries most interest you. List your top three:

1. _____

2. _____

3. _____

INTEREST ASSESSMENT

What do you really care about?

With my family:

_____

In my neighborhood:

_____

In my social circle and with friends:

_____

In my town/city:

_____

In the world:

_____

How can you help take care of the things you care about?

_____

_____

_____

What things do you want to do some time during your life?

_____

_____

_____

What industries interest you?

_____   _____   _____

_____   _____   _____

What sounds like the ideal job to you? (You may want to use a separate sheet of paper for this. The ideal job is usually more that just a job title.)

ASSESSMENT RESULTS:

Look at the results of your self-evaluation then take a few minutes to transfer your assessment results into the spaces below. This will allow you to view all of the material at once. Once you see what you have selected, you will begin to have a better feel for what work environment you prefer, what you are naturally adept at doing, and what industries interest you.

As an exercise you might enjoy checking out some of the websites listed in the appendix, or going onto a good search engine on the Internet such as **www.google.com** and trying some of the words from your skills assessment as "key words." Watch what happens! The results might surprise you and can provide some food-for-thought as to jobs or businesses you may not have considered. With these "key words" in mind, you can begin to do research that reveals areas, jobs and industries that may prove to be very promising.

YOUR LIFESTYLE AND ENVIRONMENT PREFERENCES:

YOUR NATURAL ABILITIES, TALENTS AND SKILLS PROFILE:

YOUR INDUSTRY/JOB INTERESTS:

Questions to ask yourself

You have taken the skills self-evaluation and it is hoped that you have a much clearer picture of where to concentrate your energies in searching for a possible career. In order to form/design/create a solid career plan and in an effort to prepare yourself for interviews, you need to start asking yourself basic questions that can bring your career goals into sharper focus.

Reflect on the following questions taking into consideration your completed skills evaluation. Use your answers as a basis from which to begin building the foundation for a solid plan to map your career. As you assess your skills and your expectations about a job and your career, you will be well focused. This will help ensure your success in interviewing.

Questions to consider:

1. Do you want to continue working for your current employer?

2. If so, in which capacity?

3. If so, which career path/promotional opportunities are available to you?

4. If not, what type of company or industry interests you?

5. What salary do you want (or need) to earn?

6. Do you want an opportunity with more responsibility?

7. If so, how much and at which level?

8. Do you want to have more influence over people with whom you work?

9. What type if boss do you want? What type of boss do you want to be?

10. Do you want more family or leisure time?

11. Do you want a full-time, part-time, consultant, or flextime opportunity?

12. What perks or benefits are important to you?

13. What skills do you possess that will allow you to do what you want to do?

14. What skills do you need to obtain/acquire to do what you want to do?

15. In which type of environment do you prefer working? (i.e., alone, with others, on a team; day-time hours, graveyard shift; standing/moving or sitting at a desk; dressing in a uniform, casual, or professional attire.)

There are other assessments that you may wish to pursue to help you discover what really makes you tick. It is important to do what you love! Loving what you do (almost) always ensures success. Unfortunately, as I mentioned in the beginning of this chapter, 86 percent of American workers are dissatisfied with their career choices/current jobs.

"If you don't love what you do, change what you do."

6

Doing Your Research

Any good plan requires research! You've done the assessments of your-self and the marketplace; now it's time to do the research about specific jobs and companies that offer the type of work you want. I hope that you have identified several companies to which you are interested in applying.

Now you need the inside scoop!

The more work you do up front the more apt you are to find the work you desire. With this in mind, let's go to work. There are several ways to collect data on industries, companies and jobs:

- **Contact the company directly.** You may gather information about companies in which you are interested by contacting the company directly. Often larger companies have public information or public relations departments that send out information on the company's behalf. This method is described in the Information Gathering Interview technique I have already outlined.

- **Use the Internet or local library.** Both sources offer plenty of information about public companies and industries or offer generic job descriptions. Try the Internet and start your search with a good search engine like **www.google.com.** Librarians; another resource, are trained to provide information that will point you in the right direction, and are a wonderful resource. *Note: You will also find specific references and resources in the Appendix.*

- **Ask friends or business associates.** They may have worked for companies, or in industries, or jobs you are interested in, and are another good source for gathering information.

Remember; leave no stone unturned!

Understand the jobs and positions that are available within the industry in which you are interested. It is better to discover the good, and bad of a career/industry choice beforehand, rather than after you commit yourself to an interview, a position, a company, or an industry.

Conducting your research

In conducting research, you want to uncover as much information as possible on:

1. The company

2. The interviewer

3. The job for which you are applying

The Company: There are several ways to gather information and do research on companies. With the technology we have available today it's easy to gather information about almost any company. Most small, private companies have websites, not just the large corporations. Use the Internet. It's a wonderful resource!

If you are not sure how to find a company on the Internet try a search engine (**www.google.com** is my favorite), type the name of the company, then click on "search." You will usually find their website. Another way to find a company's website is to type the company name followed by ". com". It is quite common for a company to own several URLs that point to their one web page. For example when you type **www.generalelectric.com** it takes you to **www.ge.com.** Both addresses are for the company General Electric. Another good example is Barnes and Noble, which is simply **www.bn.com** but you can also find them at **www.barnesandnoble.com.**

Methods for finding information about **Public Companies:**

1. The Internet
    *   Try **www.hoovers.com.** They offer plenty of information about public companies, or you can visit your favorite library via the Internet.
    *   Try going to a search engine and typing the name of the library along with the city where the library resides.
    *   Most states offer websites that direct you to city and/or state-specific job openings, as well.

2. Newspapers
    *   If you do not live where you are performing your job search, try the Internet. Most large city newspapers are now available on-line.

3. Library reference materials
    *   Ask the reference librarian for specific books, or try visiting the library on the Internet.

4. Employees of the company for which you are doing research
    *   If you know someone who works for the company you are researching try asking that person for the inside scoop. Remember unhappy employees give you negative information and happy employees give you positive information; in either instance the information will be somewhat biased.

Resources for obtaining information about **Private Companies:**

1. Ask for the human resources/community relations department of the company you are researching.

- If you are having a difficult time try the sales department. They are always eager to send prospective clients information about the company.

- See the Appendix for specific reference materials.

2. The Internet

- Find a good search engine. Many small and medium-sized, privately owned companies now have websites. Visit those websites.

3. The company receptionist

- This gatekeeper is also an information giver; do not be afraid to ask. Say you are going to interview soon and would like his/her help.

Gathering information about **The Interviewer:** The more you know about the person or persons with whom you will interview the easier it will be for you to relate to them during the interview. The sooner you gather the information, the more time you will have to define your interviewing strategy.

If you don't know the name of the person with whom you will interview, the best way to get that information is to call the person that set up your interview. Usually, they are happy to give you the name as well as some additional information. Explain that you are trying to prepare for your interview and feel that the more information you have, the better you can prepare. Your conversation with this person will usually get back to the person with whom you will interview. That's a good thing. You might even consider sending them both a thank you note.

When you are on the phone with the person giving you information, take advantage of the opportunity to ask a few questions about the interviewer For example:

1. How long has _____ been with the company? _____

2. Has he/she always been in this department? _____

3. Where did he/she work before coming to the company? _____

4. How many people report to him/her? _____

5. Is he/she married? With kids? _____ (Be careful here, some people don't want to share this information and you will have to judge if it's appropriate to ask or not depending on how friendly and informative the person is with whom you are talking).

6. Is he/she the person to whom I would directly report? _____

Techniques for gathering information about **The Job:** Most of us find job listings through networking and get vague job descriptions from our contacts. Some of us get job listings from job posting sources like the Internet or the classified section of the Sunday newspaper. In any case, you'll need to obtain a thorough description of the job for which you are applying. If a job definition is not easily available, ask for one! Most human resources department staff members will assist you by faxing you the details about job openings or giving you details over the phone.

7

How to Write a Resume

A resume should jump up, blow whistles and ring bells. Good resumes will make you stand out from all the other candidates. Your resume is a marketing tool, not simply a written employment history.

A crucial element of a successful job search is putting together an effective tool for selling you: the cover letter and the **resume.**

A good resume has four basic elements:

- Relevant knowledge, understanding, and expertise

- Career direction and focus

- Basic employment history describing your career accomplishments

- Education and training (especially where it supports specific jobs for which you are interested in applying)

Let me say before I go any farther that *a resume must be perfect!* Finding errors in a resume will turn off a hiring manager quicker than perhaps anything else during the pre-qualification process. In fact, research suggests that approximately 80 percent of employers eliminate candidates solely on resume spelling errors. Also, keep in mind that as you put your resume together you should focus on the employer's needs. The best way I know to do this is to ask the question, "Will this help me get the job I want?"

Assuming you are qualified for the job on the basis of at least 75 percent of the job's qualifications, answering this question correctly will most likely address the employer's needs.

Who should prepare your resume?

There are a number of methods to write your resume. You can:

- Prepare it yourself

- Use a software program designed to make resume writing easier

- Hire a professional resume writer

Before you begin laboring over a resume, you may want to consider hiring a professional resume writer to help you. When choosing a professional resume writer, keep in mind that you do get what you pay for. Make sure the professional you choose has plenty of professional experience, credentials, and references.

You should plan to pay anywhere from $75 to $500 for a professional resume. Most reputable professional resume writers affiliate with a professional association for resume writers. National associations like, PARW (Professional Association of Resume Writers) or NRWA (National Resume Writers Association). Both of these associations have websites and can make referrals in your area: **nrwa.com** and **parw.com.**

The best way to find a good resume writer is to ask your business associates, friends and family for a referral. A business associate and professional resume writer explains, "Performance is everything."

She adds, "Beware of those same friends and family members who try to talk you out of using a good resume writer by offering to help you with something like, 'Oh, you don't need to pay someone to do that. I can do it for you.'"

Remember that you will get what you pay for!

As my business associate says, "Some self-proclaimed resume writers are little more than typists and not what they say they are, and you won't know until it's too late." Be careful when selecting your professional resume writer. Make sure you work carefully with him/her and provide valuable and noteworthy information about your skills, accomplishments and work history. When they have completed their job, you will still want to run your resume by someone else for a second opinion.

Regardless how much the professional resume writer can help you, you must still provide the details from which they draw the material to create your resume. Think carefully about your background and experience.

Ask yourself about every past job: "What have I achieved in this job that will help me get the job I want?" Resume writers are trained to ask you the right questions that will provide them with the information they need to construct a dynamic resume presentation.

A good way to get your information down on paper is JobMapping™ or brainstorming your job experiences. I will discuss and outline JobMapping™ later in this chapter. It is a highly effective way to get your ideas down on paper and allows you to write effective descriptions taken from your work history accomplishments.

Before you purchase resume writing software, look around. Ask friends and business associates if they have a software package they can recommend. You might choose to go to your local Best Buy or computer store to review and select professional resume writing software. Some companies may offer a demo version to try via the Internet. Go to the Internet and check them out. If you choose to use a pre-designed resume writing software package, you will still need to outline the content of your resume and select the appropriate wording that sells you best.

What employers look for in the candidates they hire

As you begin to think about your resume, it's a good idea to know what employers are looking for. You want to highlight the traits that sell you best, and include the qualities employers are looking for in the candidates they hire. A list follows of the top qualities that employers look for in potential employees. When constructing your job descriptions for your resume, make sure you can effectively demonstrate several of these attributes.

- Articulate

- Can handle difficult people and situations

- Can set and meet deadlines/priorities

- Collaborative

- Committed

- Confident

- Creative

- Discreet

- Efficient

- Enthusiastic

- Ethical

- Flexible

- Focused

- Good communication skills

- Hard working

- Honest

- Industrious

- Insightful

- Intelligent

- Interpersonal skills

- Learns from constructive criticism

- Loyal

- Motivated

- Multitasks well

- Open to new ideas

- Organized

- Persuasive

- Positive

- Professional

- Prompt

- Resourceful

- Sales oriented

- Service oriented

- Tactful and diplomatic

- Team player

- Works well under pressure

Resume writing basics

If you choose to write your resume yourself or use a resume writing software package, there are some basics to understand that can help ensure your success.

Begin with the five "Cs" of resume writing:

- Content

- Clarity

- Conciseness

- Consistency

- Continuity

First, the **content** of your resume should be thorough without being redundant. Again, I remind you to ask yourself, "Will this help me get the job I want?"

Next, look at the **clarity** of your ideas as they relate to the way you demonstrate your objective, work history, education and other details provided on your resume. There should be a clear focus and direction as to what you want to accomplish with your resume. For example, whenever possible you will want to write a modified resume for each separate job for which you apply. Targeting your resume to a specific job will deliver much better results.

In addition, you need to be mindful of the **conciseness** of your resume material. Are the details you have chosen to include brief, yet comprehensive? They should be. The rule of thumb should always be to write clearly and concisely, especially when aiming for the always popular, **one-page resume.**

You must absolutely be **consistent** with the details of your resume. There are a couple of sound rules to follow:

- Avoid abbreviations whenever you can! Try to write out as many words as possible. There are exceptions, which include: "Blvd." for Boulevard; "Apt." for Apartment, "Pkwy." for Parkway. I recommend simply using the # sign and abbreviations commonly used in parentheses (for example, i.e. or AKA). If in doubt, write the word out; this way you won't leave any uncertainty as to its meaning.

- Follow the same format with each job description, as well as each company listing. For example, if you bold the job title on your current job, bold the job title for each job description, as opposed to highlighting the company name.

Finally, if you have organized strong **content** for your resume, written **clear** and **concise** job descriptions, and ensured that your format is **consistent,** the **continuity** or flow of your resume should be easy to follow and convincing. However, there are a few important rules that need to be mentioned, which include:

1. Always spell and grammar check your document. Your resume *must be perfect.* If it is not, don't waste your time sending it to potential employers!

2. A strong, well-written cover letter that is personalized should accompany your resume.

3. Write information in appropriate tense, particularly about job descriptions. The general rule is: present job, present tense; past jobs, past tense.

4. Avoid listing controversial issues such as religious or political affiliations.

5. When there are large gaps between jobs on your resume avoid using a chronological/dated resume, opt for a skills resume.

Having planned your resume, the next step is to do the actual work of putting it to paper. For illustrating what a good resume could look like I have added a sample resume for a secretary/receptionist. The sample resume follows the JobMapping™ section of this chapter. Keep in mind that the sample I have provided is a basic, entry-level type example. You will need to elaborate accordingly based on your own background.

When you look at the Sample Resume you will notice that it is organized in sequential order. It begins with the **Objective** or what I refer to as the "mission statement" of the resume. Your objective should be clear and concise yet distinctive. Your objective should tell the reader that you want the job being offered, have the skills they are looking for, and you are confident your skills will complement their needs. You will also want to use your objective to show how you can contribute to their success when they hire you! Keep your objective to one or two sentences, if possible.

Next, you will need to decide which you should list first, your **Education** or **Work History.** The rule here is simple:

- If you have no experience to back up your education, put your education first.

- On the other hand, if you have been working in your education-related profession for more than two years, list your work history first.

- You should list only college-level education and above. There is no need to list high school attendance or graduation.

Listing your **Additional Skills** is very important. I recommend using bullets to highlight specific skills. Bulleting makes it easy for the resume reader to scan your resume, and highlights your top abilities. I also recommend positioning your additional skills category towards the top of your resume. People who scan resumes often get no farther than the first half of your resume. Keep in mind that for each resume you send you may want to customize your additional skills category to match the job requirements outlined for the job for which you are applying.

How relevant the **Professional Organizations** are to your career will determine how important they are to list on your resume. For example, if you are a volunteer for the American Red Cross and are applying for a job as a human resources professional at a hospital it may be a benefit to you to list this affiliation. If in doubt, ask yourself the all-important question: "Will this help me get the job I want?" I want to remind you once again to not list any organizational affiliation that would be considered controversial.

On a final note, there is no need to list your references. However, you may want choose to write that your **Professional References** are available upon request. Do keep in mind that employers know if they ask for references that you will provide them. Listing them, in my opinion, is repetitive and a waste of time. Keep your references on a separate sheet and ready to hand over at the end of an interview or when an employer asks for them.

Finally, we get to write your **Job Descriptions**! You can truly make or break your chances of getting an interview by how well your write your job descriptions. Job descriptions are not merely a matter of relating information about a generic job; this is where you show yourself within a job. Here are some general rules:

- Organize your work experience. You may want to use my method of organization called JobMapping™ to help you write your job descriptions.

- Begin each sentence with an action verb or adverb (I usually remember adverbs as words that end in "ly" for example: successfully, efficiently). I've added a list of action verbs and popular adverbs in the Appendix.

- Remember, every entry into your job description should sell you for the job for which you are applying. Again ask yourself: "Will this help me get the job I want?"

How to use JobMapping™

JobMapping™ helps make writing job descriptions easier! It is the fastest and easiest way to get your thoughts and ideas down on paper.

The advantage to using JobMapping™ is that it involves a creative process and making a list of job skills does not. JobMapping™ allows you to tap into your brain's creative center to produce more usable information for your job descriptions.

Begin by setting aside an hour or so of solitary time. You can expect each job description to take anywhere from 20 to 30 minutes to create. If possible, avoid interruptions. Often an intrusion will break your train of thought and you will need to begin again. Save yourself effort and work on your job descriptions without distractions!

Once you have settled into a quiet space to work, assign a piece of paper to each job description you want to write. (Refer to Figure 1).

I recommend going back at least 10 years, if possible. If you are right out of college or do not have 10 years of work history, consider using any jobs, volunteer work, or classroom projects as potential entries on your resume to describe your experience. Leave no stone unturned! If in doubt, ask yourself, "Will this help me get the job I want?" If you are still in doubt, leave it out.

Learn to JobMap

Step 1: On the center of each piece of paper, draw a circle. In the center of that circle, write your job title.

Step 2: From the job title you have listed draw a line and add another circle. In that circle write the first job task you think of. Make notes here if what you did was unique and noteworthy. Remember you're not really talking about generic job duties but rather what you specifically did on the job that made it unique and how your uniqueness allowed you to perform your job successfully.

Step 3: Continue to add lines to connect each circle and fill in the duties that relate to that specific duty.

Step 4: Next, add another connecting line with a circle, as in Step 2. Add another job skill. Continue to add circles with items that define the job duties until you complete the sub-duties of each listed job responsibility.
Note: Do not try to force your ideas or worry about their order. Often when you are relaxed for this process you find that ideas flow easily. On the other hand, trying to force your ideas may not work as easily. This is free form thinking; do not worry about perfection at this stage!

Step 5: Next to each major circle write the letter A, B, C and so forth.

Once you have worked through each job description you will need to organize your thoughts. A general rule you will want to keep in mind while arranging your ideas is that each major circle (now labeled A, B, C, etc.) will represent one sentence or bullet point in your job description. Well-written job descriptions are usually between three to eight sentences in length. Generally the more current the job, the longer the job description. The exception here is a job that you're describing from several years prior that closely relates to the job for which you are applying.

Putting your JobMapping™ to work

Take information from your JobMap to write job descriptions. If your JobMapping™ outline has become too complicated, you can make a traditional outline like the following:

Job Description: **Secretary/Receptionist**
*(**Note:** I have used this example because most people can identify with this position and understand its requirements.)*

A. Answer phones, screen calls, and if appropriate direct caller to person. Take messages or transfer caller to voicemail if desired.

B. Dictate and write correspondence.

C. Check mail and deliver to appropriate recipient. Prepare any outgoing mail for USPS or UPS.

D. Keep President's schedule, and remind her of upcoming appointments each morning.

E. Attend staff meetings and take minutes. Enter minutes into computer and forward to meeting attendees for approval/changes.

F. Respond to emails from website for information about company and products; cc to marketing department for follow-up.

G. Manage filing of all company documents. Audit files every quarter.

H. Balance the petty cash drawer each week.

A rule of thumb here is to keep your information accurate and be honest! Employers can tell when you are padding or stretching the truth. If it is listed on your resume you should have an example from your work history to demonstrate a skill. This is a MUST!

Choose one of the two techniques listed below to write your job descriptions:

1.   Sentence style written in a basic sentence structure.

2.   Bullet style, as in the sample I have provided.

Finally, before you actually begin to construct your job descriptions you will want to use the list of action verbs provided in the Appendix. Each sentence of your job descriptions should begin with an adverb or an action verb.

About your references

It's true that most companies don't check references. However when and if they do, your references should report what you expect them to say. I cannot tell you how many references (and, yes, I always check references) I've checked over the years that have resulted in disaster when someone's supposed best friends completely discredited them.

I like to put people at ease when I check references, so I always remind the person with whom I am checking that what they tell me is confidential and will not leave my desk—and it doesn't. I am shocked at what people say about other people. I was checking a reference recently when the person speaking began to ruthlessly attack my candidate. I was stunned! I explained to the individual that what she was telling me was illegal and could potentially get her in big trouble. Wow! She quickly changed what she was saying about my applicant.

What I'm trying to get at here is this: Have someone check your references for you before you use them. Have a friend or business colleague whom you trust call your references and pretend to do a reference check. On the other hand, if you're the person for whom someone is checking a reference, be careful what you say. Don't agree to be on the reference list at all if you have mixed feelings.

About your resume's presentation

When you're finally ready to put your resume to paper there are several things you'll need to consider in terms of how your resume should look and how you'll want to have it printed. I've included some suggestions.

Chronological vs. Skills resumes

- You will almost always want to provide a chronological resume because that is the type employers prefer.

- However, if there are large gaps between jobs of more than one year you should select the Skills resume.

  - Rather than listing individual employers under an *Employment History* heading you should have two separate headings: *Employment Skills* and *Employers*.

  - The *Employment Skills* should include all relevant skills used during your career history.

- The *Employers* heading should include the various employers you have worked for and the number of years you worked for them.

  - *Note: it says number of years you worked for the employer and not the dates of employment.*

  - Adding years of service as opposed to dates will allow you to explain the employment gaps during an interview.

Layout guidelines for your resume

- Use 24-pound resume quality paper.

- Opt for a light colored paper. Speckled is popular on white or ivory. Avoid speckled if you plan to fax your resume. Faxed resumes should be on "bright white" 24-pound bond paper.

- Select a conservative look for your resume unless you're applying for a job in a creative field like graphic design.

- Use the same font throughout your resume and avoid changing fonts.

- Use basic fonts like Times Roman, Helvetica, or Arial.

- Select either 11 or 12 point for your font size; avoid any size over 14 point or less than 9 point. The best way to make your resume fit to one (or at the most two) pages is to adjust your margins.

- Margins ideally should be 1 inch around including top, bottom, right and left.

  - *If you need to take up more space* start by moving the top margin down to 1.25–1.5 inches, then move to the side margins with the same size increases as the top margin.

  - *If you need more space* start by decreasing your margins. This time start with the bottom margin, decrease to .5 inches, then decrease the side margins equally to .5 inches.

- *If you've increased/decreased your margins and you still can't tailor your resume to an acceptable length* increase/decrease your font size following the above guideline.

- *Finally, if none of the above works,* add pages when you need more space or increase font size beyond 14-point type if you need to take up more space.

  - Note: Start by increasing your name to 16 point and bolding it, then make all your bolded headings, like objective, experience, education, additional skills etc. 16 point. This will usually do the trick.

- Your resume should be single spaced with an extra space between main headings

Delivery of your resume

- The preferred choice is email. Larger companies increasingly prefer this method, and it's easier for them to keep track of and save your resume for future reference.

- Least effective is faxing. This method works if the employer requests it. However when faxed, it's hard to assure the quality of your resume.

- The traditional method of delivery is mailing which offers two options: a tri-folded version or a flat manila envelop mailing. Generally, the flat mailed version arrives neater and more professional looking and will get more notice!

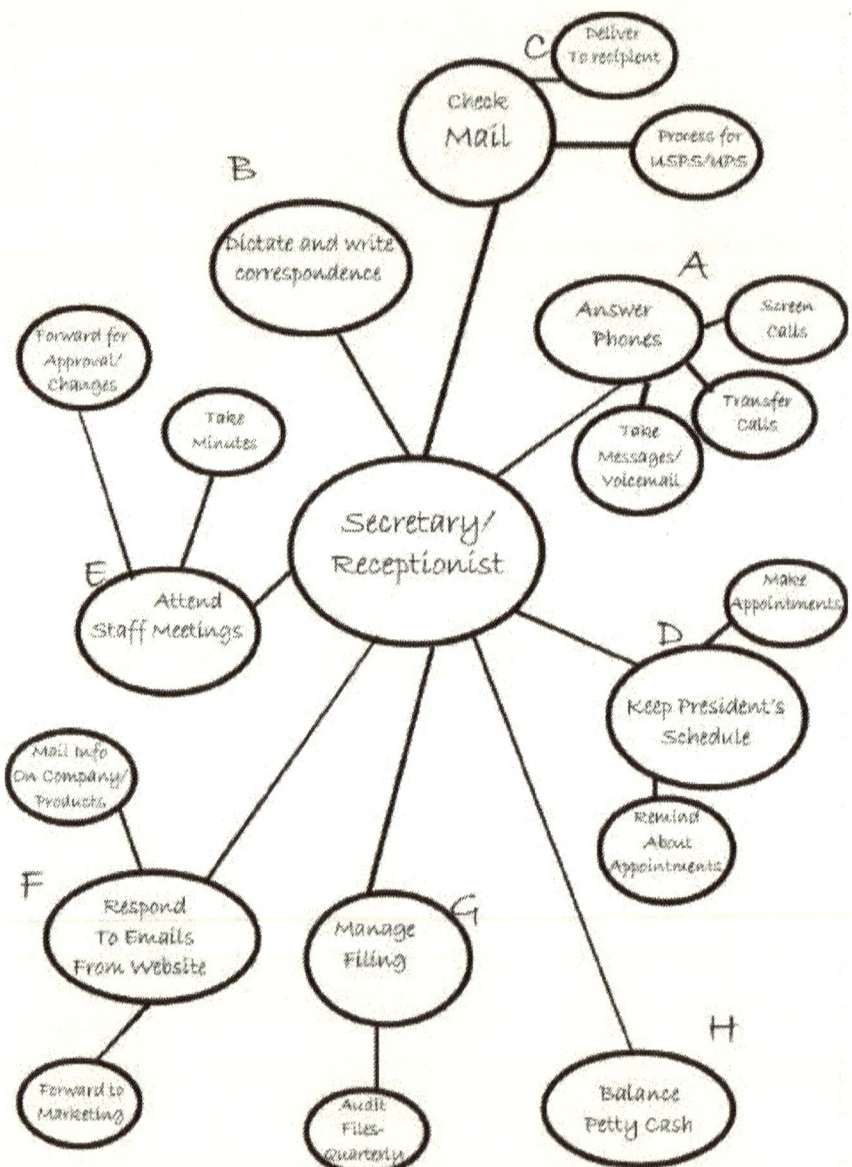

Figure 1—JobMapping™ Example

SAMPLE RESUME

ANDREA C. WOOD
1234 West Happy Street
Anytown, State 12345

Home Phone: 123-456-7890
Email Address: **acwood@email.com**

Objective: To obtain a position that allows me to use my strong organization skills in a productive environment that offers advancement opportunities.

Specific Skills:

- Microsoft Office and Windows 2000
- IBM PC and Macintosh/Apple
- Quicken, Quickbooks, and Peachtree
- MS Front Page
- ACT! Contact and Scheduling software
- Proficient with Internet Technology

- Dictation and Shorthand
- 10-Key by touch
- XEROX Copier machines
- Skilled with various FAX machines
- Lucent Telephone System
- Experienced with UPS and USPS procedures

Work History:

ABC Company   Phoenix, Arizona

Executive Administrative Assistant   July 1994–Present

- Awarded Employee of the Year, 1998 and 2000
- Efficiently answer more than 600 incoming executive calls per day and direct appropriately
- Successfully dictate and write all correspondence for six executives, using MS Word
- Manage and coordinate the delivery of all incoming and outgoing mail

---

- Developed system for mail delivery which saved the company more than $5,000

- Effectively organize and schedule President's appointments using ACT! Contact software

- Attend staff meetings, take minutes and create updates for executive team

- Enter meeting minutes into computer and forward to meeting attendees for approval and changes

- Direct all product information requests to marketing department for follow up

- Manage all files for executive department and perform quarterly audit on more than 1,500 files

- Balance petty cash drawer each week input information into QuickBooks

XYZ Company	Phoenix, Arizona
Administrative Assistant	May 1990–July 1994

- Efficiently answered multi-line phone system for five departments and 250 employees

- Managed the job activities of two part-time clerical staff including performance reviews and scheduling

- Performed updates to three departments' intranet pages

- Handled travel arrangements and scheduled appointments for marketing and executive team

Education:

Anytown Community College	Anytown, Arizona
Associate of Arts in Secretarial Studies	August 1991
International Association of Administrative Professionals	
Certified Professional Secretary (CPS)	January 1992

Professional Affiliations:

- Member International Association of Administrative Professionals

- Member American Business Women's Association, Corresponding Secretary (1999–2000)

- Volunteer Trainer for American Red Cross CPR Program

Considering an eResume

There are several resume posting sites on the Internet. The large majority of them allow you to post your profile free. You will find several resume posting sites listed below and in the Appendix. Most sites allow you to fill in the blank or check an appropriate box that applies to your employment history and expertise. A word of caution: check their confidentiality clause. Most sites give you an option to remain anonymous. You certainly don't want to post a resume only to have your current boss see it the next day!

Many companies ask you to submit a resume they can scan. Ask for the specific parameters for their scanning system. Many are bold and uppercase character sensitive. You need to know their requirements so your resume won't be eliminated on a technicality.

It's important which format a company is looking for. If you don't know, ask! Do not assume that they want a Word, WordPerfect, or an AmiPro document. You will need to know which version their system will recognize in case you have a more advanced version. If in doubt, call and ask. If you are unable to contact the company before sending your resume, send your perfectly crafted resume in the text body of an email, and include your resume as an attachment.

Posting your resume on a website

Here is a list of the Websites where you can get help creating and even posting your eResume and professional profile:

- **www.csn4jobs.com**

- **www.monster.com**

- **www.resume.com**

- www.tbrnet.com

- www.resumenet.com

- www.jobweb.org

- www.jobstar.org

- www.10minuteresume.com

- www.provenresumes.com

- www.jobweb.com

8

How to write effective cover letters

Cover letters can be tricky! Employers often ignore cover letters. However, if used properly they can be valuable tools. I recommend that you always include a **cover letter** explaining your reason for submitting your resume. It serves as an introduction, highlights your specific qualifications and objectives as they pertain to the job for which you are applying, and demonstrates your written communication skills.

Though I do not recommend using a canned cover letter, I have included an example from which to work. Make your cover letter personal and professional. It should be concise and easy to read. I have included two types of cover letters:

1. **Informational Response** cover letter

2. **Two-column Comparison** cover letter

Both are very effective in reaching your audience—the hiring manager.

Generally, the first person to see your cover letter is a secretary in a human resources department. That person, trained to eliminate resumes, will take less than one minute to do so! Make your words count!

Other uses for cover letters:

- As a follow-up after an interview to thank the interviewer, to re-emphasize your skills, and summarize your match for the job.

- To cover anything you may have forgotten to mention during the interview.

- To initiate networking with your contacts.

Informational Response Cover Letter—Content Sample

Date

XYZ COMPANY (Use all uppercase letters for the company name)
Attention: Ms. Jane Smith
Re: Executive Administrative Assistant to the President
123 East Company Street
Anytown, Arizona 12345

Dear Ms. Smith:

I was very interested to see your advertisement for an Executive Administrative Assistant to the President in the Sunday Edition of the *Anytown News.* I have been seeking just such an opportunity; I believe my background and the job requirements are a good match. Enclosed please find my resume for your review and consideration.

Of particular note for you and the members of your team as you consider your employment opportunity for Administrative Assistant to the President are my strong accomplishments in **meeting deadlines,** and **successfully organizing and coordinating schedules.** These skills closely parallel the qualifications you outlined in your advertisement.

Consider the following:

- Awarded Employee of the Year, 1998 and 2000
- Management responsibility for all part-time clerical staff
- Certified Professional Secretary (CPS) by the International Association of Administrative Professionals
- More than 11 years of successful Administrative Assistant experience

After eight years with the ABC Company, I have a thorough understanding of every aspect of the function of an executive administrative assistant. My current employer is very happy with my performance. However; with the recent downturn in the semiconductor industry, I am eager for new challenges that allow me to use my strong skills in a more stable industry.

If you are seeking an executive administrative assistant who stays current in her field, who understands technology, who earns one hundred percent staff support, and who is as career-committed as it takes to achieve total success, then please consider what I have to offer. I would be happy to have a preliminary discussion with you to see if we can establish a mutual interest. I will call you within the week to answer any initial questions you may have, and to hear about your hiring process.

Thank you for your attention to these materials. I certainly look forward to exploring this further.

Yours truly,

Andrea C. Wood
Phone: 123-456-7890
Email: **acwood@email.com**

Enclosure

Two-Column Cover Letter—Content Sample

Date

XYZ COMPANY (Use all uppercase letters for the company name)
Same as previous sample

Dear Ms. Smith:

I was very interested to see your advertisement for an Executive Administrative Assistant to the President in the Sunday Edition of the *Anytown News*. I have been seeking just such an opportunity as this, and I believe my background and your job requirements are a good match. Enclosed please find my resume for your review.

Of particular note for you and the members of your team as you consider your employment opportunity for Administrative Assistant to the President is my strong performance in **meeting deadlines,** and **successfully organizing and coordinating schedules.** This closely parallels the qualifications you outlined in your advertisement.

Outlined Job Duties/Requirements	My Related Experience
1. 5+ years Administrative Assistant experience 2. Excellent Communication skills 3. Organized and detailed oriented 4. Experience with Lucent Phone system 5. Light bookkeeping duties	1. 11 years solid Administrative Assistant experience 2. Excellent communications skills both verbal and written, dictate and write all executive correspondence 3. Responsible for CEO's appointments and scheduling 4. Eight years progressive experience with Lucent 670 Phone system 5. Ten years experience with Quicken, Quickbooks and Peachtree software. Currently balance weekly petty cash

After eight years with the ABC Company, I have a thorough understanding of every aspect of the function of an executive administrative assistant. My current employer is very happy with my performance. However; with the recent downturn in the semiconductor industry, I am eager for new challenges that allow me to use my strong skills in more stable industry.

If you are seeking an executive administrative assistant who stays current in her field, who understands technology, who earns one hundred percent staff support, and who is as career-committed as it takes to achieve total success, then please consider what I have to offer. I would be happy to have a preliminary discussion with you to see if we can establish a mutual interest. I will call you within the week to answer any initial questions you may have, and to hear about your hiring process.

Thank you for your attention to these materials. I certainly look forward to exploring this further.

Yours truly,

Andrea C. Wood
Phone: 123-456-7890
Email: **acwood@emailcom**

Enclosure

Practice

*Confidence, like art, never comes from having all the answers;
it comes from being open to all the questions.*

—Earl Gray Stevens

9

Traditional Interview Q & A

As if you haven't been busy enough gathering information and assessing your background and skills, now you need to spend time preparing and practicing the answers to your interviewing questions.

As I've said, no two interviewers are the same. However, most interview questions are. When employers interview you, or any candidate, they want to determine three things:

1. **Can you do the job?** In other words, do you have the skill set to get the job done?

2. **Will you do the job?** What the interviewer is looking for is whether or not you are motivated to do a good job.

3. **Can you get along with co-workers?** Interviewers want to know if you are a team player. Are you a troublemaker?

Because interviewers don't ask these questions directly, you need to understand that every question they do ask is designed to address and answer one of the above questions. There are many questions that you should anticipate and prepare to answer.

Before the interviewer begins asking questions, take advantage of the **three minute, three question rule.** This rule is your way to let the interviewer know that you're interested in answering questions for them. You need to execute this rule within the first three minutes of your interview. Ask the hiring manager: "What three qualifications do they most want in the person they hire for the position?" Go on to explain that your reason for asking this question is to ensure that your answers allow you to address their most important concerns.

Once you have settled the question about what the interviewer really wants in an applicant, you're ready to begin answering the questions. Below is a list of the top, traditional questions asked during an interview and the information employers wish to elicit from you based on your responses.

The most frequently asked interview questions

Take some time to evaluate how you would answer each of the following questions. I cannot provide you with specific answers because your answers will be unique to you. What I have provided for you is what the employer wants to find out about you by asking certain questions and what you might consider answering as you develop a convincing strategy. Remember to use examples that illustrate your experiences, and qualify and quantify your answers. Describe your accomplishments and practice your answers out loud with a friend or in front of a mirror.

1. What are your most important accomplishments or what was your greatest success?

    • Take information from your accomplishments exercise in chapter 5.

2. Tell me about yourself, or how you would describe yourself.

    • Give professional information and avoid personal information.

    • Provide details and examples that paint a picture of a positive "can-do" team player.

3. Describe your ideal job. What are you looking for in a position?

- This answer should not include anything that drifts too far from the job description for the job for which you are applying.

4. What things would you like to avoid in your next job?

   - *BE CAREFUL WITH THIS ONE!!! Make sure your answer doesn't include comments that imply negative things about your past boss, co-workers, or company.*

   - Also, make sure you don't mention anything that is listed in the job description.

5. Why have you left or why do you wish to leave your current position?

   - A safe answer includes a statement about growth potential or opportunity, unless your company is going through a lay-off, or something similar. You'll want to explain the situation.

6. What do you think of your supervisor/current employer?

   - Avoid saying anything negative!

   - Stress the points you like about your current supervisor/ employer and if you don't have anything positive to say, think up something neutral like, "He/she does his/her best to support our department and staff."

7. Does your current supervisor know you are planning to make a change?

   - Answer truthfully.

   - If a current supervisor does not know you're leaving the interviewer will assume you're unhappy in your current situation and will ask questions about why you're leaving.

   - If your current supervisor does know your leaving, the interviewer may check with them for a reference.

8. How did you get along with your boss, co-workers, subordinates?

    - ALWAYS answer with a positive answer, like "I work well on teams and get along well with co-workers."

    - Give examples if possible.

9. How would you feel about working with someone younger, opposite sex, etc.?

    - ALWAYS be okay working with someone different than you. It really shouldn't matter.

    - If it does matter, don't tell the interviewer but wait until you have an offer and make your decision then.

10. Do you work well under pressure? Are you willing to work overtime, travel, etc.?

    - Provide examples of times during your work history where you have done all of the above.

    - Give honest answers about how much you're willing to travel as a percentage, for example 25 percent.

    - Express that you are open to working overtime if required but add that you hope that by working efficiently you can keep overtime to a minimum.

11. What has been your greatest failure?

    - It's okay to have a failure. Make sure you can provide a positive and effective solution to overcome or fix your failure.

    - Give examples.

12. You have never done this type of job before. What makes you think you can succeed?

    - If you have great experience, give examples.

- If not, find examples from your work history, school experiences and volunteer work that closely parallel the job for which you are interviewing.

- Illustrate the similarities and show enthusiasm for learning something new.

13. What are your short, medium, and long-range goals?

- Avoid answers like "owning my company" and "moving up to management." Instead, use answers that show consistent progress, opportunity for growth, challenge, and reasonable salary increases.

- Show assertiveness with your career strategy but avoid overly aggressive goals.

- Your goals should align with the job for which you are applying.

14. How do you spend your free time? What do you read?

- This is not the time to proudly boast about a religious or political volunteer project or controversial topic and/or book. Stick to something generic or self-help oriented, something current and interesting.

- For fun, you might say something humorous like "I just read *'Help! I Need A Job'*."

Set aside some time to consider each of these questions. Your answers should "paint a picture" by using positive examples from your work history, school work or volunteer activities. *Keep your answers to less than two minutes.*

* Question #2 is what I call the **"elevator speech."** Perfect this answer through lots of thought and practice. Think of yourself on an elevator going from the lobby to the 10th floor. You have about 2 minutes to sell yourself to the person riding in the elevator (the hiring

manager). Make your two minutes count! Be concise, be thorough, be interesting and be memorable!

Additional questions to prepare for

Below is a list of more traditional interview questions that you should prepare for. Set aside the time to prepare appropriate answers. Rehearse your answers but do not memorize them. Practice with a friend and ask for their honest critique. Have them make notes and suggestions. When considering your answers remember to think of examples that positively paint a picture of you and your strengths.

1. What specific goals other than those related to your occupation have you established for yourself for the next ten years?

    • Your goals should align with your career objective and the job for which you are applying.

2. What do you really want to do in life?

    • Be reasonable but be enthusiastic—after all, it's your life.

    • Add something fun and ambitious.

3. What have you done to find a job?

    • Mention the standard methods, like classifieds and the Internet.

    • Make sure to mention using your network. This shows your resourcefulness.

4. How do you plan to achieve your career goals?

    • Have a plan laid out, or at least one in mind.

    • Be reasonable, assertive, and make sure your goals align with the job for which you are applying.

- Try to demonstrate goals that would allow you advancement within the industry of the company with which you are interviewing.

5. What are the most important rewards you expect in your business career?

   - It's perfectly all right to show lots of enthusiasm here. Just keep it aimed towards the job you want for a particular interview.

   - Let the interviewer know that you want a job where you can use your strengths and abilities to make a difference.

6. What do you expect to be earning in five years?

   - The amount should be reasonable and within the expected parameter of potential advancement (see formula below).

   - If you're not sure how much that is, add 5 percent per year (the standard percentage for annual salary increases) to the starting salary. For example 5 percent of $30,000 is $1,500 (.05 x $30,000=$1,500) extra income per year. You would add about $1,500 per year to the $30,000 which would be $30,000 + 6,000 (which is $1,500 x 4 years = $36,000). You could say $36,000 to $40,000 per year.

7. Why did you choose the career for which you are preparing?

   - This is a good time to make mention of your self-assessment and career profile.

   - Give reasons and examples of why you love your profession that illustrate your success.

8. Which is more important to you, the money or the type of job?

   - Your answer should always be job satisfaction.

- If you're in sales you want to say job satisfaction is important, but every good sales person will tell you money talks!

9. What do you consider your greatest strengths and weaknesses?

   - Think of your cheat sheet! (your 3"x5" card that lists A. your three strengths; B. a weakness and how you've overcome it; C. the accomplishment for which you are most proud).

   - Have strengths that align with the **three-question, three-minute rule** from the beginning of this chapter.

   - Have examples of how knowing your weakness allowed you to learn from and overcome it.

10. How do you think a friend, colleague, or professor would describe you?

    - Use your elevator speech response.

11. What motivates you?

    - This should be a two-fold answer—one career-related and the other family-related. Focus on you career-related motivators.

    - Be passionate about what motivates you.

12. How has your college/educational experience prepared you for a business career?

    - Good answers include statements like "How to stick with something," and "by providing a well-rounded exposure to many different situations."

    - Employers want to hear specific examples from your school experience and activities that demonstrate your enthusiasm for your career.

13. Why should I hire you?

- Think of your cheat sheet!

- Have strengths that align with the **three-minute, three-question rule** from the beginning of this chapter.

- Give specific examples that show why you would be a good fit for the job.

14. What qualifications do you have that make you feel you will succeed in business?

   - Use your strengths and refer to your career plan.

15. What do you think it takes to be successful in a company like ours?

   - This is where your homework pays off. With the right preparation, you know something about the company and the interviewer. Use this information to show your interest.

   - Interviewers look for answers that tell them you are dedicated, passionate, hard working, goal oriented, loyal and that you have leadership potential.

16. How can you contribute to our company?

   - Use the answer to the **three-minute, three-question rule** here.

17. What qualities should a successful manager possess?

   - This response typically describes the type of manager you would be.

   - Good answers include: encourages growth, leads and mentors, or delegates responsibility.

18. Who was your favorite manager? Why?

   - Similar to above.

19. Who was your least favorite manager? Why?

- Use caution here.

- Don't bad mouth past supervisors. Try to be diplomatic and honest.

20. Of which accomplishment are you the most proud? Why?

    - The answer to this question is on your cheat sheet.

21. Which subjects in school did you like best? Why?

    - Your answers should align your skill set with your chosen career and the job for which you are applying.

    - Provide examples of school projects where you used skills that you will use in the position for which you are interviewing.

22. Which subjects in school did you like least? Why?

    - This question can relate to your weakness.

    - Try to use an example of overcoming a particular challenge in the class and what you learned by conquering the problem.

23. If you could change something about your past, what would you choose?

    - This is not the time to unveil your shady past. Don't bring up emotional or personal issues.

    - Use mistakes you made in high school or college. We all have skeletons from our college days. Keep your example legal and on the humorous side, if possible.

24. Do you have plans for continued study? An advanced degree?

    - Make sure your response would benefit the employer. If not—don't mention it. Say that you are undecided.

25. Do you think that your grades are an indication of your ability?

- If you had good grades, say yes.

- If you had bad grades say no, with an explanation about how you're not a natural student and have always had to work for grades and that you're better with hands-on projects.

26. What have you learned from participating in extra-curricular activities?

    - More and more companies are putting weight on the importance of extra-curricular activities to a well-rounded employee.

    - Give examples from your work and school activities that illustrate lessons learned that could be applied to the work environment.

27. In which type of work environment do you prefer working?

    - Let your observation skills pay off here.

    - Your answer should reflect your true preference while incorporating your observations about the company work environment.

28. How do you work under pressure?

    - When you answer, give an example of a school or work project where you were under pressure and how you handled the situation in a positive manner.

29. In what part-time or summer jobs have you been most interested? Why?

    - This response should provide an example of a part-time job that relates to the job for which you are applying.

30. Why did you choose to seek employment with this company?

    - This is a good time to mention your research.

31. What do you know about our company?

- Here's where you sit back, and smile and thank the job-hunting gods for your good fortune for having done your research.

- The personality of the interviewer will tell you what information is important to them. For example, if they are an accounting type, give them numbers and stats. If they are a marketing type, give them ideas that show your creative side.

32. What two or three things are most important to you in your job?

- I think it's fun to use humor here and say, "What were those three qualifications you mentioned early in the interview."

- If humor isn't appropriate, make sure your response aligns with the job qualifications and the research you've done on the company.

33. Are you seeking employment in a company of a certain size? Why?

- If you have a strong opinion here, don't bother interviewing with companies that don't fit your preference.

- If you don't have a preference regarding company size, say so and mention that you're open to the best career opportunity.

34. Do you have a geographic preference? Why?

- Be honest. If you love warm winters, don't interview for a job in North Dakota.

35. Will you relocate? Does relocation bother you?

- If you are willing, say yes.

- If you are not willing, say no.

- Companies pay lots of money to relocate new employees. Don't say yes unless you really mean it. If you're not sure, explain that you're open to relocation for the right offer.

36. Are you willing to travel? What percentage of time are you willing to travel?

    • Be honest. Don't say you will travel and later change your mind.

    • When you give a percentage state a range, such as 25 to 50 percent of the time. Later, you can hold to the lower amount if you need to.

37. What major problem have you encountered and how did you deal with it?

    • Use your weakness.

    • Provide an example and how you overcame that challenge.

38. What have you learned from your mistakes?

    • Answer should be similar to above.

Having perfect answers to interview questions is always stressful. It's impossible to give anyone the perfect answer because each interviewing situation is different. The best advice is to practice. I always recommend practicing, but not memorizing.

Candid not *canned*

I've had more than one hiring manager tell me they can tell when a candidate has planned his interview question responses so well that his answers feel and sound canned. Hiring managers appreciate the applicant who has done their homework and cared enough to put some thought into their interview, but I've never met one who liked canned answers. It is important to know how you wish to respond to the questions above, to be prepared with good examples and thoughtful answers. That's why you practice. Don't memorize answers.

Have you ever heard someone who has memorized a speech or someone who read a speech word-for-word? It's obvious they have either memorized their material or they are insecure with the delivery of their words. In either case, the speaker is in jeopardy of forgetting what they memorized or losing their place in the speech. To know what you want to say and be able to say it candidly is the best approach to successful interviewing. That way you won't freeze if you forget what you are supposed to say.

Can the canned answers!

What about trick questions

A friend of mine, who is a hiring manager, points out, "Avoid asking trick questions. It shows little about the person (being interviewed) and shows a lot about you (the interviewer)."

I've found that most employers don't like asking trick questions. In fact, 88 percent of the hiring managers I interviewed said they don't have trick questions, don't use them and don't recommend using them. Those who do ask trick questions say what they do is watch for non-verbal responses to deceptive questions. Almost everyone I talked to can relate to being put on the spot only to find out that they've been tricked. It's no fun and most employers don't want to scare you. They want to determine if you're a good match for the job.

A trick question is any question that puts you on the spot that you could not possibly have prepared for. Some examples might include:

1. What is your favorite color? Why?

2. If you could be any animal which would you choose and why?

3. How do you feel about _____? (sometime these can be unintentional, illegal questions)

4. Which U.S. President (or famous person), is your favorite and why?

I've actually had interviewers ask me these questions, and some of my candidates report that they have been asked them. If you get a trick question, do your best to answer it. Be honest and if possible interject some humor into your answer. If someone asked me my favorite president, I'd have to say the current president. History is just not my thing! Don't be intimidated if you can't think of an answer. Just tell the interviewer you've never thought about whatever they asked you and ask to move to the next question.

The mock interview

After you have carefully considered how you will answer questions, make them unique to you and appropriate to the type(s) of jobs you are seeking and feel comfortable with your delivery of each response. It's time to practice. Practice with a friend or business associate you trust. Sitting on the sofa reading and reciting questions and answers with a buddy won't do. You need to simulate as closely as possible an interviewing scenario. Your mock interview needs to feel serious. You should make the mock interview seem true to life by dressing as you would for an actual interview and preparing as you would for the real thing.

Have your appointed interviewer give honest feedback. If you choose a friend who will only give you glowing praise, find another friend for this project. Ask your chosen mock interview partner to take notes, make suggestions, and to offer sincere but constructive advice.

Following the guidelines in this chapter and practicing will greatly increase your chances for positive consideration and recognition when going through the interviewing process. Practice does make perfect, as the old saying goes. Just make sure your responses are candid and rehearsed, not memorized. I have talked to many hiring managers who can detect and loathe a canned response. They are usually turned off by answers that are too perfect.

Though there is no guarantee, I can say with confidence that if you practice and rehearse your responses, your chances for success will dramatically increase.

10
Behavioral interviewing

Unlike traditional interviews, behavioral interviewing allows a candidate to use real stories to demonstrate successful and not so successful work and school history. Behavioral interviewing is a dynamic method of interviewing chosen by more and more employers. It is designed to show that candidate's past job experiences usually predict future job performance.

When planning to do a behavioral interview the interviewer begins by identifying the desired skills and behaviors being sought for a particular job, then structures open-ended questions and statements to elicit detailed responses revealing information about a candidate's work history and experience. A rating system is then developed. This system evaluates a candidate's performance based on selected criteria, which the employer has identified and is searching for during the interview. As the candidate being interviewed, you should be prepared to answer the questions and statements thoroughly. Keep in mind with each response that you must ask these three questions and answer accordingly:

1. Which _situation_ from my work history successfully demonstrated what the interviewer is asking?

2. What _action_ did I take to effectively handle the situation?

3. What was the _outcome_ that followed?

Think of your answer as following this linear model:

Situation → Action → Outcome

A business associate whom I greatly admire for her expertise in human resources and with dynamic interviewing systems models her company practices for interviewing methods and procedures. She offered this advice for candidates: "Keep in mind that the employer is looking for a pattern of the way you solve problems. He/she believes that past actions predict future results. If you do not have a specific work related situation, tell them so and relate the answer to the way you tackled a challenge in school."

She adds, "Do not gloss over the answer by saying 'That's never happened to me, but I think this is the way I would handle it...' Behavior event questions are written so that every candidate can relate it back, just like a story. Generalized answers come across too bookish, so try to be specific."

It's a good idea to think of specific work or school related experiences that "sell you" well. Think of situations that you performed at or above expected levels and where you felt proud of the work you accomplished or goals you achieved. These examples will offer the interviewer the "story" they are looking for that shows your ability to perform successfully on the job.

Below are a series of specific areas employers may want to explore and the desired response they wish to elicit. First let's take a look at an example:

- Question from interviewer: "Describe a situation where you found yourself dealing with someone who did not like you. How did you handle the situation?"

  - The <u>situation</u>: Subordinate complains that you're too happy in the morning and you find that they are talking behind your back.

- The <u>action</u>: What did you need to do/have to start tackling the problem? How did you get the tools in place to start working on this issue?

  - Evaluate the situation and realize that you may threaten the other person. When working on projects "tone down" your demeanor so they are more comfortable. Pull them aside and tell them someone told you that they were talking behind your back, (giving them the benefit of the doubt) and tell them it was probably a misunderstanding on the other person's part. Ask them to please let you know if something is bothering them, so you can work through challenges together.

- The <u>outcome</u>: Person's attitude changed, they were more open to discussing their issues, and were more comfortable on a day-to-day basis working together.

<u>Customer service focus:</u> Considering the feelings and needs of others, as well as perceiving and responding to the needs of your internal and external clients.

1. We've all dealt with difficult people at work; give an example of this from your work history. Why was this person difficult? How did you work with that person?

2. Describe a situation where you felt left out or disliked by co-workers. How did you handle the situation?

3. Tell us about a time you went above and beyond the call of duty for an internal customer or co-worker. What was the situation and what specifically did you do? Why was this considered "out of the ordinary"?

4. Describe the most difficult customer service incident that you have had. How did you handle it and resolve the situation to ensure the customer's satisfaction?

<u>Your ability to learn quickly:</u> Applying new information that relates to the job.

1. Which methods have you learned that help make your work or school easier? How did you learn that method?

2. Tell us about the methods you use to learn a new skill, for example, book reading, on the job training, etc. What was the last new skill you learned, and how long did it take you to master it?

<u>Your planning, scheduling and organizing (time management) skills:</u> Establishing a course of action for yourself, others, and projects that allows you or a team to accomplish goals.

1. How do you set your priorities? Give examples of your tactics, time management, scheduling priorities and projects.

2. Tell us about the types of tools you use on the job to ensure that your work is completed on time and accurately—for example, checklists, daytimer, Palm Pilot, etc. Also, what types of events can cause you to completely re-prioritize?

<u>Your ability to adapt to new or different circumstances:</u> Adapting to new or different situations, people, and environments.

1. Tell us of a transition from one job to another. How did you adapt to your new work environment?

2. Tell us of an event where you had to adjust quickly or spontaneously to a change over which you had little control. How did you handle the constant job changes, and what did you do to prevent stress?

<u>Your ability to motivate and take initiative:</u> Monitoring the ability to proactively self-motivate and inspire yourself and others to achieve goals.

1. Give an example from your work or school activities that were satisfying. Describe those episodes that were not satisfying.

2. Tell us about your favorite supervisor. What made this person so positive to work for, and what was the synergy between the two of you?

3. On the flip side, tell us about your least favorite and why this person was difficult to work with.

4. Take us through a recent project, either at work or at school, that you completed. From inception to completion, walk us through the steps of identifying the problem, researching the best outcomes and methods to finish the project, and how you deployed the solutions. What was the outcome? Was it on time? Was it under/at budget?

Your work ethic, values, and standards: Setting high goals and principles for yourself and co-workers regarding work ethics and moral code.

1. Tell about a time when you performed above expected standards of performance.

2. Describe times when you were dissatisfied with a co-worker's work performance.

3. What have you done in the past to achieve or meet successful standards?

4. Have you dealt with a difference of opinion with a co-worker about what standards of ethics on the job or on a project should be? How did you handle that?

5. We'd like to ask this question for self-reflection: Tell us about a time that you made a mistake. What was the situation, and most important, what did you learn from it?

Your ability to work on teams: Effectively working with others on teams, or on group projects.

1. Describe a situation where others you were working with on a project disagreed with your point-of-view, ideas, or methods. What did you do to resolve the disagreement?

2. Discuss a time when a co-worker(s) was not doing their part in contributing to a project. How did you handle the situation? What did you do to help resolve the issue?

3. Show a time when you had to arrive at a compromise with a co-worker or team members. What did you do to positively resolve the issue(s)?

4. Describe a situation where a team member talked to you negatively about another team member. What did you do?

5. Describe a situation where you had a conflict with another team member or co-worker. With whom did you discuss the situation? What did you do to attempt resolving the situation or fix the problem? Did a supervisor assist to resolve the situation? Did you agree with the supervisor's methods for resolving the conflict?

Your ability to communicate: Expressing concepts and information in writing and speaking.

1. If it applies, give me an example of a presentation you gave. How did you prepare? With whom did you work to complete the presentation? What steps did you take to prepare the presentation?

2. Give me an example of when your listening skills paid off.

3. Talk about the written project for which you are most proud. Give an example of a speaking presentation, or worthy verbal project.

Your ability to solve problems: Find practical and effective solutions for challenges and problems.

1. What steps do you use when solving problems before making decisions?

2. Describe a situation where you identified a small problem and resolved it before it became a larger problem.

3. Discuss a time when you had to resolve a conflict without the benefit of a supervisor's input.

How you manage people and projects: Managing people and projects.

1. In a supervisory or leadership role, have you had to discipline or counsel a subordinate or team member? What steps did you take to discipline the individual(s)? How did it make you feel? How did you prepare for the confrontation/meeting?

2. Describe a situation where you had to resolve a conflict between two strong-willed employees or team members. What steps did you take? How did you prepare for the situation?

3. Describe your biggest failure as a manager. What did you learn from that mistake? How has it helped you become a better manager?

Your professional knowledge and technical skills: Understanding industry and technology.

1. Describe a situation where you felt "out of your league." When did you realize you were in "over your head"? What did you do to resolve the situation?

2.   Discuss a situation where you had to ask for assistance on a technical aspect of a project. To whom did you go for help?

3.   Describe a time when you used prior knowledge or experience to solve a problem.

4.   On a scale from 1 to 10 with 10 being the highest, rate yourself on the following: Word, Excel, PowerPoint, Access, Project, (or any other appropriate software for any particular job).

Remember, your answers to any question should paint a picture that portrays you as the best candidate for the job. When you prepare your answers in advance, it gives you an opportunity to think about your work history and how you can use specific examples from that history to sell yourself. Another benefit of thinking about your responses in advance is that if an employer asks you a question not listed you will have spent enough time exploring your background to not get caught off-guard.

11

Illegal interview questions

It surprises me how many people are not sure which questions are okay to ask during an interview, and which are not. I am also one of those individuals. Because of this, I keep a reference book on my desk and try to attend seminars to stay abreast of the often-changing legal and illegal question gallery.

Most of you know some of the illegal questions which employers are not permitted to ask at any point during the interviewing process. Many more of you are uncertain which questions are fair game and which are not.

To help you, I have asked for the guidance of an expert in this field. She offers several suggestions that may help you identify specific areas, which interviewers may or may not cover, and where the line is drawn so you can determine if the questions are legal.

Lisa[*] offers some additional suggestions as to how a candidate could answer a question that is not job related:

1. I'm sorry, but could you explain how this question relates to my individual job performance?

2. Is my _____ (martial status/parental status, sexual orientation, race) essential to your knowing how I would perform in this position?

Interviewers can sometimes ask illegal questions without knowing or realizing that they have done so. Usually they have not meant anything by an illegal question and just asked out of ignorance. If you respond, as Lisa suggests above, the interview can continue without a defensive tone and the interviewer is forced to re-think about why he/she asked the question.

Lisa adds, "The interview isn't over until you have left the building." Many employers have been reprimanded because the manager asked "casual" questions while giving a candidate a tour or walking him or her out of the building. When the candidate wasn't chosen, the manager had proof that he/she didn't judge the candidate based on the answers provided during the inverview itself, and some forget they even asked an improper question.

Dos and don'ts regarding illegal interviewing questions: *

Subject	Lawful Inquiry	Unlawful Inquiry
Name	Have you ever worked for this company under another name?	If your name has been legally changed, what is your former name?
Age	Are you over 18 years of age? If hired, can you furnish proof of age?	Any question that tends to identify applicants age 40 and over.
Citizenship	Do you intend to reside permanently in the US? If you are not a U.S. citizen, do you have the legal right to remain permanently in the U.S.? What is your Visa status?	Are you a citizen of the U.S.? Are your parents/spouse citizens? On what dates did you, your parents/spouse acquire citizenship?
National Origin/Ancestry	What languages do you speak, read or write fluently?	What is your national origin/ancestry? What language is spoken in your home? What is your native tongue?

Dos and don'ts regarding illegal interviewing
questions: (Continued)*

Subject	Lawful Inquiry	Unlawful Inquiry
Race or Color	NONE	Any question that directly or indirectly relates to race or color.
Religion	NONE	Do you attend church services? What religious holidays do you observe?
Gender	NONE	Do you wish to be called Miss, Ms. Or Mrs.? Do you plan to have children in the future?
Marital Status/Relatives	What are the names of relatives already employed by the company?	Are your married? With whom do you reside? Do you have children/ ages of children?
Physical Condition	Do you understand the requirements of the job, and can you perform them? Do you need any accommodations to perform the job?	Do you have any physical disabilities? What is your disability, and what caused it? Have you had any serious illnesses? What is the prognosis of your disability?
Education	Questions related to academic, vocational training or professional education of an applicant, including schools attended, degrees/diplomas received, graduation, courses of study.	Any questions asking specifically the nationality, racial, or religious affiliation of the school.

Dos and don'ts regarding illegal interviewing questions: (Continued)*

Subject	Lawful Inquiry	Unlawful Inquiry
Experience	Questions related to applicant's work history, questions related to applicant's military service.	Questions related to years of service in the military. Veterans have protected status.
Character	Have you ever been convicted or a crime? If so, when, where are disposition of cases?	Have you ever been arrested?
Work Schedule/ Traveling	Would you be willing to relocate? Are there any reasons why you would not consistently arrive for work according to the company's work schedule?	Any questions related to childcare, ages of children, or other subject construed as discriminatory, particularly by women.
Miscellaneous	Statements or notice to applicant that any misstatements or omissions of significant facts in written application forms or in an interview may be cause for dismissal.	Any inquiry that is not job related or necessary for determining an applicant's potential for employment.

*   The above table was provided by Lisa Elowson, business associate and behavioral and illegal interviewing expert.

12

Questions you should plan to ask the employer

As we have discussed, interviewing is a two-way exchange. However, the person being interviewed often forgets that they have a responsibility to ask questions during an interview. Interviewers expect you to ask questions about the job, the company, even the people with whom you will work. Having well thought out questions planned prior to the interview is a must. Below are several questions you may wish to consider asking the interviewer.

Questions about the job:

1. Is there a job description I can see?

    -   It is hoped you already have a job description in hand.

2. What are the three most important qualifications for this position?

    -   Always ask this question during the first three minutes (remember the **three-minute, three-question rule**).

    -   As I've said, the answer to this one question will give you the focus for the rest of your answers. By that, I mean employers will tell you what is important in the job and you'll know what they are looking for.

- You should use the information and examples from your work history to demonstrate parallel definitions from the company's job description and top qualifications.

3. What are the main responsibilities of this position?

  - This is the **three-minute, three-question rule** again!

  - Ask as soon as possible during the interview, preferably during the first three minutes.

4. Where does this position fit in the overall organization?

  - You may even ask to look at the company's organizational chart. Most companies have them and they will help you see where you would fit in, in the general scheme of things.

Questions to save for the right time: (Keep in mind that at the end of an interview the interviewer will probably ask if you have any questions).

1. What is the growth plan of the company?

  - Most interviewers are happy to discuss this with you and welcome questions about their company's growth and expansion.

  - There is one exception, and this is where doing your research pays off. It is when the company is going through a financial reorganization or bankruptcy that has been negatively publicized in the media. In this case you should let the employer bring up this issue.

  - However, companies undergoing financial stress can offer tremendous opportunities to learn and advance your career skills. Weigh your options carefully and learn to trust your instincts.

2. Who are the major customer/competitors?

- I hope you have done your research! It will give you an opportunity to ask specific questions about what you've learned.

- If you have not been able to find much information about the company, now is a good time to ask. Most employers are happy to share this information and many will tout their company's superiority.

3. What are the prospects for advancement?

- This is usually covered by the interviewer during the first interview. It is appropriate for the interviewer to bring this up. However, if they do not by the end of the interview, ask. It will show that you are interested in the position.

- If it is obvious that the next promotional level would be the interviewer's position, do not ask about advancement. At this point it will work against you rather than for you.

- You may want to confirm potential advancement with a comment like, "It sounds like the next move from this opportunity would be into _____."

4. What are the employee benefits?

- Again, this is usually answered by the interviewer.

- If they do not bring it up during the first interview, it is better to let it go until a subsequent interview.

- If benefits are not mentioned by the second interview, you should ask. Either the interviewer has forgotten they haven't covered benefits, or the company does not have a benefit package to boast about. In this case you should consider what your minimum benefits requirements are.

5. What are the policies regarding salary increases and promotions?

- Wait to let the interviewer set the tone/pace for this question. Generally it is not a good idea to bring up salary during the first interview. However, there are two exceptions:

  - The position is an hourly and/or an entry-level position.

  - There is quite a discrepancy within the market for the particular position for which you are applying. For example, I know of companies in the same industry that pay as much as $10,000 less per year as starting base salaries for sales staff.

Closing questions:

If you don't have a business card from the interviewer, now is the time to ask for one. If you have interviewed with more than one company representative, ask for their cards as well or at the very least, for the correct spelling of their names.

Below are other questions you should consider asking toward the end of your interview.

1. What is the next step?

   - What you are actually asking here is, "Will there be a second interview?" The always-dreaded answer is "We will get back to you."

   - If you sense their enthusiasm, try to schedule your second interview.

2. When will the hiring decision be made?

   - If they don't mention it, ask.

   - Often the hiring manager and/or the interviewer will give you a clear indication of when you should expect to hear back from them.

3. How well do you feel my qualifications match your needs?

- How an interviewer answers this questions will give you quite a bit of insight into how interested they are in you.

- Pay close attention to how vague the answer is. Usually, the more detailed they are the more interested they are in you.

4. *Last but certainly not least,* ask for the job!

   - You can say something like, "I want this job," but a more effective response might be, "If the job's mine I can start on _____," or try "So when do I start?" (Stop talking and wait for the interviewer to answer. It will be the longest wait of your life, but it will be worth it.)

   - If you do ask for the job, chances are you'll get an offer. Seriously! Employers say that when someone asks for the job, that they feel they must be interested in the job. Nine out of 10 candidates who do ask for the job get it, or at least they get a second interview.

   - Asking for the job shows that you are interested.

   - Just make sure that if you ask for the job you really want it!

13

Questions about salary, compensation, and offer negotiations

You've evaluated the company and advanced to the final interviewing stage and are certain you're going to get an offer. Preparing for the offer and the subsequent salary negotiation can be as important as preparing for the employment interview. What you know beforehand will set the stage for success or failure. Know as much as you can about the company's potential offer, your status and how you feel about the opportunity. Usually if an offer is forthcoming, a company representative or hiring manager has given you information that hints of a pending offer. You may not have all of the answers but you can go into any employment negotiation understanding the process and what you want to accomplish from the experience.

Have a plan and work your plan.

Prior to the negotiation interview

Here are points to consider before the salary negotiation:

1. Sell yourself. Understand how to sell your strengths and how your strengths match the job for which you are applying.

2. Learn job worth/range. What's the competition pay range for similar positions.

3. Evaluate the benefits and policies. Are they sufficient for your needs?

4. Consider your objective and minimum requirements. Knowing your minimum requirement helps you to determine your bottom line. Look at your budget and consider your career plan.

5. Gather information about the position requirements and determine how you stack up. You may want to begin your offer comparison before the offer negotiation. This will give you a feel for how viable the offer actually is.

It's important for you to bring up questions about the salary first, before the interviewer mentions compensation. Once the initial negotiation begins, and the interviewer informs you of their intent to offer you a position, try to continue the conversation with something like, "Now that you are aware of my qualifications and accomplishments, what salary do you feel is fair for the position we have been discussing?"

Avoid starting answers with "I need…" A more candid response from you will illicit one of two responses:

• The first offer may result in a higher offer.

• Or the interviewer may say, "Sorry, that is the best I can offer."

In either case, you must remain calm and inform the interviewer that you would like to take some time to consider the offer. You actually will want to take time to consider an offer. Never accept an offer on the spot if at all possible. However, for lower level positions, the interviewer expects you to accept immediately. It is always okay to say you'd like to think about it until the next day. If you make your decision sooner, by all means call the company back immediately.

Questions to anticipate during the negotiation interview

1. "What were you making at your last job?"

- If you know what they might offer beforehand, you can plan better how to respond to this question.

- Avoid bringing up past salaries in an interview. When asked, indicate that your old salary and job belong to a different job and company and probe for the range they have in mind. For example, "I don't want to prejudice my position with you by being too high or too low; could you tell me more about the range you have in mind?" An alternative is, "I'm very interested in working with your company and salary won't be an issue."

  a. Be careful with this second response. It may lock you into a salary that is far below what you anticipated and the employer may come back and say, "You said that salary wouldn't be an issue."

  b. If this is a completely new career field for you and you really want to be in "this" new field then the second response is more appropriate.

- If the interviewer insists on specific salary information, one of two rules apply here:

  a. If you want a higher salary than they are offering, elaborate on your prior compensation package and benefits, overtime, bonuses, commissions or any other point that bears mentioning. Answer with something like, "My salary, including bonuses, is in the high 50s. I am expecting my annual performance review soon and expect to be at something in the low 60s." In other words, describe your total compensation package, not just your salary.

  b. If on the other hand you need to come down from what they are offering (usually due to a total industry/career change), downplay your prior compensation package, using something like, "My base salary was in the low 50s primarily because of my tenure in the industry. I understand that changing industries/careers will certainly have an effect on the salary I can demand. With that in mind, I am open to any fair and reasonable offer."

2. "What salary are you looking for?"

- First, ask for the salary range and then relate your experience and accomplishments to that range without being too precise. You might say, "With my qualifications for the position, what compensation level do you feel is appropriate?"

- Try not to come across as playing a game, but rather as trying to gather information to help you make an informed decision.

- Finally, when considering your answer you may want to add, "I feel that the opportunity is the most important issue, not the salary. If we decide to work together, I'm sure you'll make me a fair offer." Then add, "I'm open on the salary issue because I am very interested in working for your company and I can see a good opportunity here for both of us."

Negotiating the offer

Employers don't base salaries on your bills or financial obligations but rather on job qualifications and how important those qualities are to the financial bottom line of the company. Remember that most companies offer salaries less than what they are willing to pay. They usually expect you to make a counter offer. However, if the offer is acceptable the first time around, say so and move on to a discussion regarding benefits.

If the offer in not acceptable (keep the market in mind) ask to think the offer through and be sure to schedule another meeting to conclude the salary negotiation. If you choose to counter-offer, reschedule the next meeting within two days or as soon as possible.

Here's the formula I recommend when considering the offer and what you want. Take their offer and the difference between that and your salary requirement and add the difference to the salary you want. For example, if you want $50,000 and they offer $47,000 ask for $53,000. The difference between $47,000 and $50,000 is $3,000. Add $3,000 to what you want and ask for $53,000. Often hiring managers counter offers and meet you half way from what you want and they initially offered allowing you to get the salary you desire and their salary to stay in an acceptable range*.

Carefully consider the final offer and if necessary ask for 24 hours to make your decision. If they offer you what you asked for, they will expect you to take the offer. If you still need time to consider their proposal, explain that their offer is generous and that you need to discuss it with your significant other or that you simply need to think about it overnight. Be prompt with your response.

A note of caution: if you are considering several employment offers, be honest. Let the hiring manager know that you have other offers and how much time you require to consider all of your options. If you are in a high-demand industry, most hiring managers do not mind this request and will respect your wishes. If on the other hand you are holding out for another offer with a more desirable company, let the hiring manager know you will need some time to think the offer over.

In the meantime, contact the other company and let them know you have another offer. Tell them you are most interested in working for them but that another company is expecting your answer soon. It pays to be honest here, as well.

If you are a top contender, the employment manager will usually tell you your rank or your realistic chances for getting the position. Depending on the answer, you will want to respond accordingly as soon as possible to the other company.

*Note: If you are using a company's offer to get your current company to give you a raise or promotion, you are making a huge mistake that may have devastating results. Once you have used this method to get a raise or promotion your supervisor will remember this and most people have little respect for game players. You may get what you want initially, but in the

big picture you hurt yourself and management will label you a disloyal game player.

Observation

Without speculation there is no good and original observation.
                                                    —*Charles Darwin*

14

Calming your fears

You have done the groundwork. You've prepared; you've practiced; now you're ready to execute your plan.

After your careful preparation, the perfect resume, practicing your interview questions, and the extensive research you have done on the companies, jobs, and hiring managers—you're ready to take the next step. You're ready to go on an interview and you're nervous. Even the most prepared interviewees get nervous.

Avoiding the pre-interview jitters

If you are nervous about your interview, join the club!

Nervousness is natural! Everyone has feelings of nervousness at one time or another, and like you most people get the jitters before an interview. I have never met a candidate that has not been nervous at some point. The interviewer expects you to be nervous and they too can be on edge. After all, they want to find the best candidate. They have something at stake. They need to find the right person and they are responsible if that person works out or does not work out. Being nervous is a sign that you care.

However, being too nervous is a sign that you are either not right for the job, are unusually shy, or unprepared for the job interview. You can avoid all three by planning.

To avoid being overly nervous during an interview, try the following:

1. Be prepared.

2. Believe in yourself. Write down the reasons you are right for job and why you want it.

3. Allow plenty of time to arrive at the interview. Arriving early puts you at ease and allows you to relax and observe before your interview.

4. Practice relaxation. Breathe deeply while waiting for your interview. Being prepared and arriving on time will help you accomplish this.

5. Remember, this is not the only job in the world. Often people think that they must have or get this job. They feel defeated when they don't do as well as they expected during an interview and don't get a second interview call-back. Remind yourself it's only one job and it isn't the only job. If this job doesn't work out, keep trying until the right job does come around. I've found that not getting a job is often a wonderful stroke of luck when you get a better job offer later that is more suited to you and your strengths.

6. Have your cheat sheet safely tucked in your jacket, pants, or skirt pocket. Just knowing it's close will usually help you to remain calmer.

At the risk of sounding like a broken record, I reiterate the importance of being prepared and stress again that the more work you do up front the more apt you are to get work. Preparation offers confidence. Confidence opens doors and closes deals.

Being ready for an interview is your greatest defense against nervousness.

What you have to offer a company and being able to effectively demonstrate those skills during an interview will usually put you in the final running for any job opportunity. This self-knowledge often helps reduce the level of stress you experience going into an interview.

Controlling your nervousness

However, if your nervousness just won't go away, try these techniques. I've recommended them to many candidates over the years to help them calm down before and during an interview. As you arrive at the interview allow plenty of time to park, meet the receptionist, and look over your notes and cheat sheet, which I describe below.

To help relax, use the following techniques:

1. **Deep breathing**. Breathe in for a count of eight and out for a count of eight. Actually count to eight. What this does is helps your mind to focus on something else, something mundane and simple. Take five to ten deep breaths, depending on how nervous you are and how much time you have. I sometimes use this method myself and will often incorporate thinking of a cool color like blue or green. Both colors are relaxing and remind me of a placid lake or fresh spring grass.

2. **Gentle hand pressure**. I learned this method while in college. I was taking a public speaking class and our professor suggested using this method. I love talking to crowds, but I can tell you I've had an occasion or two in which this technique benefited me. Try it. When you feel nervous or stressed during an interview try pressing your hands together, while they rest in your lap, to a count of two to four. As you release the pressure, your muscles will relax and send a message to your brain to relax as well. The nice thing about this method is that it is not visible to anyone with whom you are interacting.

When you feel extremely stressed and cannot seem to calm yourself, remember honesty is always the best policy. Let the interviewer know. Tell them you are qualified for the job but that you feel overly nervous because you are very interested in the job and want to do a good job interviewing. Ask them if you may get a drink of water. At this point, you may want to say something humorous if you can think of something, like: "I always get nervous when I haven't had enough water. I just hope my jelly legs will get me to the water fountain."

Laugher and smiling are a good defense to nervousness and tension. It is pretty hard to pass up a sincere smile and an honest request for help.

If you are still nervous, ask yourself why. Are you normally this nervous during interviews? Do you want this job too much? Evaluating why you are nervous will help you not to be so nervous. You may want the job and you may really need the job but try to remember that it is not the ONLY job!

If you are desperate, if you really need the job, the employer will know. If you are too nervous, they will wonder why as well. The best defense to nervousness is to be prepared so you will not have anything about which to be nervous.

Visualize your way to success

Businesses train their employees to use visualization to improve performance and production. Coaches use visualization with athletes because research has shown that mental rehearsal is an effective way to increase athletic performance. Students use visualization to improve test scores while therapists use imagery to enhance relaxation skills.

Dieters imagine a thin and beautiful body. Medical scientists have watched the power of mental imagery increase the immune system as well as lower a person's blood pressure and heart rate.

Visualization techniques can help many areas of your life, including interviewing. If you practice visualization, you will likely find that your interviewing skills improve. Here's how visualization works for athletes:

- First, research has shown that imagery strengthens neural pathways and certain movements. When you perform a certain task or skill through mental rehearsal your muscles fire in sequence as they do when they are actually performing that skill.

- Second, imagery helps athletes formulate a "mental blueprint" which helps make movements more familiar and automatic.

- Finally, the imagery is so vivid and realistic that the central nervous system becomes programmed for success.

Mental rehearsal can be carried out virtually any time and research suggests it works. Try this visualization exercise:

- Find a cozy spot and get comfortable.

- Begin with deep breathing and general muscle relaxation.

- Think about the mindset you want to carry with you into your interview.

- Connect with the goals of your interview (i.e., knowing where to go, arriving on time, looking polished and professional, answering questions easily and knowledgably, connecting with the hiring manager, etc.).

- Use positive goal-oriented affirmations ("I am thoroughly prepared for this interview. I look professional and am able to answer questions easily and provide details that will show the hiring manager that I am highly qualified for this position.").

- Project self onto a large video screen:
  - See yourself getting ready for your interview.
  - As you arrive at the interview, see yourself being received by the hiring manager/interviewer with a smile and making a great first impression.

- See yourself answering questions easily and demonstrating your strongest skills.

- See and feel yourself in different situations (i.e., your initial meeting with the hiring manager, meeting with co-workers and other office personnel).

- See and feel yourself in command, in control, and confident and enthusiastic at the interview.

- See others you interact with at the interview responding to you with enthusiasm and interest.

- See yourself getting a job offer and rewarding yourself for a job well done!

It's important to remember that everyone gets nervous before an interview, even those people who are usually very confident in an interviewing situation. What matters is not whether you're nervous but how you handle your nervousness. Learn the techniques used by the most successful people help you calm your fears before and during your interview.

15
The interview

It's funny. Now that you're actually at the Interview, you really don't have much left to do. You've done the hard part. Granted, you'll have to spend some time observing the company environment, people, and the interviewer, but since you know what to look for, you really don't have much to do but relax and enjoy the interview. Easier said than done.

As if I haven't preached enough about preparing, now I need to mention that there are additional tasks to accomplish before your interview. Actually the day before your interview, if possible. They are:

1. Drive by the company location so you won't have difficulty finding your way on the day of the interview.

2. Phone the interviewer to re-confirm the interview time. By now, the interviewer has received your confirmation note in the mail and will be impressed that you've called and followed up as well.

3. If you haven't already inquired, now is the time to ask what type of interview to expect including the number of people with whom you will interview.

4. Decide which outfit you are going to wear. Make sure it is clean and pressed.

5. Before your interview, you should review your cheat sheet. Go over the interviewing dos and don'ts listed below, as well as the checklist. You may have already heard a list of dos and don'ts for interviewing, but the list always bears repeating or reviewing, as does an interviewing checklist.

The interviewing checklist: things you should do, be, or have

- Detailed job description of job for which you are interviewing

- Information about company, including address and phone number

- Information about the person with whom you will interview

- Receptionist's name at that company

- Professional resume

- Cheat sheet

- Business card resume

- Portfolio with notebook and pen for taking notes at the interview

- Professionally dressed (light on top, dark on bottom)

- Professionally groomed (simple accessories, nothing extreme)

- A great attitude with a pleasant smile, good eye contact, firm hand-shake

- Ask for the interviewer's business card before you leave

- *ASK FOR THE JOB!*

I am an organizer at heart. I like to have everything laid out the night before. I even have two sets of makeup for traveling so I can be out the door in a flash and organized to boot. I'm not suggesting you have two of everything. However it's a good idea to have everything ready before you need it. You'll have less stress this way and less stress means better interviewing.

When organizing the night before an interview, check your list and make sure everything is ready to go. Have directions to the interview on a sticky note along with your portfolio notebook. I recommend for both men and women keeping a small, clear zipper bag, (clear works best so you can see what's inside) in your vehicle with some basics like breath mints, sticky notes, aspirin, clear fingernail polish (for those nasty pantyhose snags that plague women), fingernail clippers/scissors, five dollars (for unexpected parking expenses), and a small mirror (just in case you have broccoli in your teeth).

You will also want to keep your portfolio notebook loaded with resumes, a pad of paper for notes, a pen and pencil, business cards (when appropriate), your quick reference phone number book, a city map and your cheat sheet (with extra 3"x5" cards for new and improved versions).

I hope you're not laughing! I'm serious about the zip bag in your car and your loaded portfolio, because there is nothing more frustrating than planning to arrive on time and to be running late for an appointment because you can't find something important you need to take to your interview.

Once again, here it comes…prepare, prepare, prepare!

Take a couple of minutes and read over the interviewing dos and don'ts. Most of the tips will be information you may have heard, but as with all good advice it bears repeating.

Interviewing dos

1. Send interview appointment confirmation cards (email or mail depending on amount of time until your interview)

2. Be prompt, and arrive at least 10 minutes early

3. Listen attentively and take notes

4. Express ideas clearly

5. Be brief and to the point (keep answers to 2 minutes or less)

6. Act confident as well as enthusiastic

7. Pay attention to body language (see chapter 16 for more details)

8. Answer question with examples

9. Relate positive experiences

10. Ask appropriate questions (prepare some in advance)

11. Stress your qualifications

12. Be factual

13. Think before you speak

14. Be prepared

15. Smile and make appropriate eye contact

16. Give a firm handshake

17. Always, always send thank you notes within 24 hours

18. Dress professionally and appropriately

19. Have extra copies of your resume

20. Have a current cheat sheet and business card resume

21. Ask for the job!

Interviewing don'ts

1. Talk too much (take 2 minutes or less to answer any one question)

2. Answer yes or no; elaborate appropriately

3. Talk about politics, religion, personalities, or controversial topics

4. Name drop

5. Say you can do anything

6. Argue

7. Criticize the interviewer

8. Complain or gossip about your current or past employer(s), supervisor(s), or co-workers

9. Talk about personal problems, relationships, or family

10. Wear "funky" too loud fashions (review chapter 4 on appropriate dress)

11. Bring up salary (interviewer should mention salary first)

12. Smoke or drink alcohol during a luncheon interview

13. *Forget* to ask for the job!

Recently a friend who was hiring for a middle management position at his company told me of a candidate who showed up an hour early for his interview. When my friend went early to get the applicant for the interview, the candidate was dressed sloppily, didn't have a copy of his resume and started the interview talking about a recent family crisis. My client later told me later in an exasperated tone, "Why did he even show up early, just to be so unprepared? He should have stayed home and gotten ready!"

If you're going to go to the trouble to show up for an interview, plan to be ready. Plan to know what to do and what not to do.

16

Tips of the trade

Knowing what to observe

When asked, "What is the first part of oratory (speaking or speech-making)," Demosthenes, the famous Athenian orator and statesman, answered "action." The second he replied was "action." When asked what was third, he still answered, "action."

People tend to believe actions more than words.

You've probably heard the saying, "It's not what you say but what you do that people remember." During a communicative exchange, especially during an interview, what we respond non-verbally often contradicts what we say aloud. Most of us spend 75 percent of our waking hours communicating. Eighty percent of that time is dedicated to "listening" to non-verbal chatter.

As the listener, we tend to put more weight on what we see than on what we hear. You can understand how important non-verbal communication is to the interviewing process. Defining the different areas of non-verbal communication will help you during an interview to antici-pate what to expect and how to react accordingly.

This is my favorite area of interviewing. Feeling what you hear. Trusting what you see.

When asked, 75 percent of employers first noticed non-verbal aspects of a candidate before they noticed anything else. Actually the first "conversation" in an interview is usually non-verbal; it's the 20-second **halo effect** period I talked about in chapter 4. Of the 75 percent of employers who recognized the non-verbal behavior of candidates, 38 percent said they first noticed eye contact, 25 percent observed the candidate's smile, and 12 percent the candidate's body language. The remaining 25 percent of respondents observed appearance, confidence/demeanor, and energy level/attitude/enthusiasm as being crucial to their impression.

Those critical 20 seconds really do make a difference. If you understand what to do with your non-verbal observation time and learn how to use non-verbal clues, you can often direct the course of your interviewing success.

Let's take a look at the critical areas of **non-verbal** communication. Non-verbal communication includes:

1. Facial expressions (smiling, frowning, expressions of surprise and anger, etc.)

2. Eye contact (direct, lacking eye contact, too much eye contact)

3. Tone of voice (inflection, loudness, softness, stuttering, or accents)

4. Body posture and motions (crossed arms or legs, fast-paced gait, dragging of feet, slumped shoulders)

5. Tension and energy level (anxiousness, tired/lethargic, strung-out)

6. The position we take within groups (withdrawn, draws attention, follower, leader)

During the interview, **what you observe**, what you see, hear, and feel, is the basic formula for success!

What we observe (see, hear, and feel) + **how we use it = how well we do in the interview.**

Literally the difference between success (getting the job) and failure (not getting the job) depends on what you observe. Watch! Watch everything. Observe all the minutiae of the environment, the people and really get a "feel" for what you see.

In this chapter, I am going to discuss and outline what I call the **tips of the trade**. This is my passion.

These tips are actually nothing more than keen observation, which allows you to *tip the scale in your favor*. If you have done your homework, you will already know something about the company and the person with whom you are to interview. Beyond that, the things you will want to pay close attention to include:

1. The waiting/reception area. Is it neat and tidy, or messy?

2. How is it decorated, or is it decorated?

3. Is it quiet, or noisy? Do you hear music? What kind of music?

4. Are the people smiling and interacting with one another?

5. Does it smell pleasant, or do you notice something unpleasant?

6. Are there pictures on the wall and what do they reveal?

Watch what's happening. Would you want to work here?

Let's take a closer look at the **reception area**. What you observe in the reception area or lobby of a company will tell you a lot about how the company is managed, what's important to management, and how the people who work there feel about their jobs and each other.

People usually smile when they're happy. Offices are tidy and organized if it is important to the management. Often in their waiting areas, companies will display pictures of the community events they support and awards they have won. Take a look around; really absorb what is happening. Try to get a sense of the tension and/or energy level of the workers. What you see may provide you with information you may use later during your interview. What you discover in the reception area will undoubtedly tell you what is important to management, as well as how well received management is within the company.

One of my favorite clients, a furniture manufacturer, has an owner that puts his people first. When I toured his facility, he proudly showed me the manufacturing area and pointed out the dust free environment (quite uncommon with furniture manufactures) and the pale yellow walls which he proclaimed looked much better than the traditional dull gray. He stated the color was actually a better shade for the mental health of his workers. He believed it was more cheerful and he wanted happy employees. The first candidate he hired from me was a human resources manager and he hired the candidate to "make life better for my employees." What a great manager! What a wonderful company, with pale yellow walls to boot!

Trust, loyalty and good business start at the top.

After observing the surroundings ask yourself how you feel. Learn to trust your instincts! This next question is going to sound odd—but how does it smell? Think about the times when you have been in a situation where the smell was unpleasant. Could you work all day in a place that smelled bad? You might get used to the smell but you might not. Are the odors common to the company or industry? Are the smells potentially toxic? If not, what are the smells?

Sometimes the smells are magnificent. I had an experience once while touring a client's facility having to do with wonderful aromas. As I pulled into the parking lot, I recognized the delicious scent of fresh baked goods. My client manufactured mouth-watering pastries. What a fantastic smell! During the tour I asked my client how he could work there day after day and not weigh 2,000 pounds. He laughed and replied that, "After a while you get used to anything."

He didn't smell the pastries anymore. He had even tired of sampling them! I can't believe that. In any case, not all smells will be pleasant; some will take getting used to. What you recognize (and determine you can tolerate) will be important.

Remember the question about music? Do you like elevator music, what about country music? Remember that what you hear in the lobby is what you will most likely hear all day long. Of course, you could invest in an inexpensive portable stereo to listen to your choice of music.

All the details count. Pay attention to everything, everywhere.

Meeting the interviewer

You will continue your keen observation when you meet **the interviewer.** Pay attention and make the same observations as before in the reception area. When a situation is right you feel it. Remember the halo effect from a few pages back. Not only will the hiring manager have an immediate feeling about you but you will have distinct feelings about them and the company, as well. Do not ignore those feelings when evaluating an opportunity.

It is important not to judge too harshly at first, but give yourself some time to look around and get a feel for what is happening. Once settled in the interview, ask yourself these questions:

1. Do you like the interviewer?

2. Are you comfortable (some nervousness is expected), and do you like the environment?

3. Would coming to work here make you feel energized and enthusiastic?

Within the first couple of minutes in the interviewer's office, take a quick look around. What you see should make a big difference as to how you answer. If you are not taken to an office but rather to a conference room, pay close attention to how the interviewer is dressed. The same criteria they use to judge you is the same information you will want to use in deciding about them. How are they dressed? Are they well groomed and organized? If you are normally a well organized, well groomed person you probably would not be comfortable working with, or for, someone who is not.

If you are taken to their office, look closely. Observe the placement of the items on their desk. Are the objects on the desk placed parallel to edge of the desk or at an angle? Usually, people who place objects on their desk parallel to the edge are detailed oriented, and people who place items on their desk at an angle are more creative and free-thinking. This is a general rule, but one that you can usually count on.

As you can see in the diagrams below the desks are very different. That's because the occupants have different personalities. Can you guess which of the two is more detailed oriented?

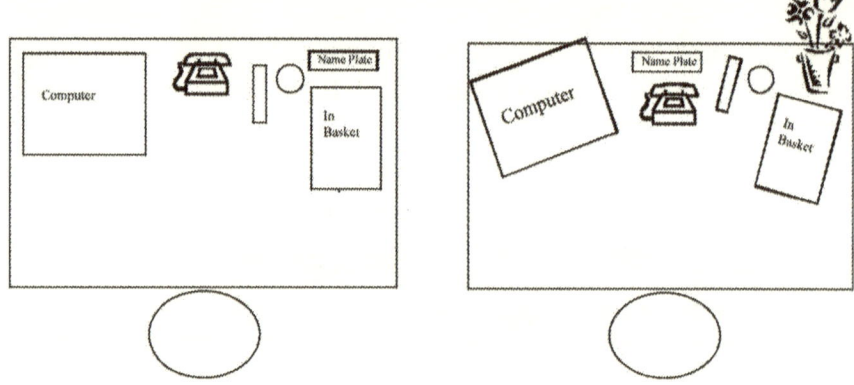

As you look around the interviewer's office, ask yourself these questions:

1.   With what types of items do they decorate their office?

2.   Do they have pictures of family?

3.   Do they have expensive artwork?

4.   What about clutter on their desk, or orderliness? All of these things will tell you something about what is important to the person with whom you are interviewing.

Remember, the information you gather as you observe can be used as a conversation ice breaker, or as a way to relate to the interviewer.

Some of the general assumptions might include:

- What is important to people will be displayed in their office environment.

- How important orderliness and organization are will be portrayed by how orderly and organized the papers are on their desk.

Remember, these are general assumptions. Some of the most organized people will have completely messy desks during the day. However, most organized managers will tidy their desk before an interview!

Maybe at this point you are thinking, "Why should I care how organized they are, or how they are dressed? I just want a job."

I understand this, but I would ask you to consider, "Can you work for someone long term that has basic traits that are very different from you, or that you don't like?"

If the hiring manager seems organized and you want to learn to become more organized, then the particular environment may be great for you. On the other hand, if you are organized and the person with whom you will work and report to is not, you may find yourself becoming very frustrated.

You should remember, how you feel during an interview will amplify how you feel after employment.

If you interview in a conference room or another room that is not the private office of the interviewer, watch how they place papers or coffee cups in front of them. Detailed individuals might tap paper edges on a table for perfectly flushed ends where a more creatively oriented person might spread papers across the desk.

People generally hire people for one of three reasons:

1. They like the person.

2. They are like the person (have something in common with them).

3. They believe the person can help them be more successful.

With that said, another important aspect of interviewing is being highly sensitive to the way in which an interviewer asks questions. Most questions provide an opportunity for an interviewer to use the word "think" or "feel."

For example, a question may start something like, "Tell me how you **feel** about _____?" On the other hand, you may hear, "Tell me what you **think** of _____?" Chances are the question seeks the same basic response. However the personality of the interviewer often dictates how they will ask a question.

The two different types of interviewers are identified as **thinkers and feelers**. Much like the scenario with the desks, thinkers and feelers have different personalities as well. Generally, the thinkers will have the "Type A, Attention-to-Detail" desk and the feelers will have the "Type C, Attention-to-Creativity" desk.

As you answer questions keep in mind that "feel" implies that there is room to change your mind. It is more emotionally charged and "think" is more definite. When you "think" something there is usually less room for change, and if you do change your mind you can come across as wishy-washy or perhaps as being someone who is easily influenced by someone else's opinions.

The point here is not only do you need to observe how an interviewer's offices appears but you also need to listen to how they ask questions and how certain words impact your answers. In an interview, intent listening should start from the second the person reaches out a hand and states his/her name and last until the ending handshake. Good listening skills allow you to answer questions on a level that will allow the interviewer to best relate to you and your answers.

When you take the time to listen to questions, you get a clue as to how to answer them. For example, when a thinker asks you what you "think" of something, tell the interviewer what you "think." On the other hand, when an interviewer asks you how you "feel" about something, answer by telling them how you "feel" about that particular topic. What this keeps you on the same wave length as the interviewer.

Another effective technique is **mirroring**. Mirroring is simply that—mirroring behavior. If you watch what the interviewer does while interviewing you can get a feel for how important something is to them. Here's what you can watch for and what it generally means:

Behavior or Action	What it means
Leaning forward	Interest or enthusiasm
Leaning backward	Relaxed, or non-committal
Crossing leg toward door	Ready to end interview
Crossing arms over chest	Closed to what you are saying
Nodding head up and down	Agreeing with your statement

To mirror an interviewer's body movements, move as he or she moves. For instance if they lean forward, you lean forward. This forces you to pay attention to them and what they are doing. Be careful to not spend so much time mirroring that you can't answer your questions effectively. When you mirror the hiring manager's body movements, what you are telling them is two things:

1. I am interested in what you are saying.

2. I am like you, and we have similar interests.

I've had people comment to me when I was mirroring their body movements, "I feel so connected to you. It is like you are really relating to me." Usually I am, because I am paying attention to their body behavior. You can do the same thing. Pay attention to the way the interviewer is positioning his/her body and match that movement. When they lean forward, you lean forward. When they lean backward, you lean backward in your chair; but don't lean too far back. You don't want to tip over!

Avoid posturing yourself by crossing arms or legs, even if the interviewer does. You do not want to give them the impression that you are not interested, or that you are ready to end the interview. It is helpful for you to see and understand these behaviors because it clues you into how well "received" you are by the interviewer.

My favorite *tip*

I like to save the best for last. My favorite tip is simple but extremely effective. By using this tip, I can almost promise three things that will change the interview:

1. You'll have the information to answer every question in the interview.

2. You'll have a leading edge.

3. You'll get a second interview.

Here's my **favorite tip**—the three-minute, three-question rule that I've already discussed in chapter 9. Ask the interviewer what's important to them so you know what information to give them when you answer questions. Ask the question "What are the three most important qualities that you are looking for in the candidate you will hire for this position?"

Bingo! This is where expert listening skills will make or break you. Listen carefully, watch intently, and pay very close attention. When the interviewer answers this question for you, he/she will literally give you the material from which to answer every other question during the interview. It's that simple, but it's that critical too. Use the information you get from the interviewer's answer to respond honestly to his/her questions. Look for solid examples from your work/school/personal experiences, or past successes that positively demonstrate the "most important qualities" that are important to the interviewer. Don't be dishonest or make up experiences, or you'll find yourself in an uncomfortable mess. Avoid using "would do" or "could do," but use specific examples of what you really did. Use the "most important qualities" information to help the interviewer more closely identify with you and let your experiences prove that you are the right person for the job.

As an example, let's say the interviewer tells you the three most important qualities for this position are:

1. Having the ability to *meet deadlines.*

2. Being able to successfully *manage a project team.*

3. Being *resourceful.*

Let's take the above qualities and apply them to some of the basic interviewing questions we've discussed.

1. What qualities should a successful manager possess? Examples from your work history might include:

    *   Detailing how you met deadlines on important projects and reports

    *   Establishing how you directed the efforts of team members by recognizing their strengths (resources) and using those positive attributes to successfully accomplish projects

    *   Describing how you were resourceful in finding solutions to challenges on projects and with people

2. What have you done to find a job? Examples of your resourcefulness and creativeness in finding a job might include:

    *   Illustrating how you creatively and resourcefully worked your network through information gathering interviews and asking for referrals

    *   Explaining how you organized your job hunt, kept track of it (your contact information form) and set and met specific goals and deadlines for a successful job search

3. In which type of work environment do you prefer working? Examples that might prove successful include:

- Explaining that your experience has been that positive work environments produce exceptional work habits, which generate excellence in the workplace

- Showing how your contributions to an organization improved the work environment and morale

- Describing projects you spearheaded or volunteered for that made your work environment more positive

You should be able to provide several examples from your work history that easily and effectively demonstrate your ability to do the job and meet the specific qualifications that the interviewer has identified during the three-minute, three-question rule period. The techniques outlined here allow you to simply apply your knowledge regarding your past work history to any interviewing situation. These techniques will help you ask questions, listen to the answers, and finally deliver what the interviewer wants to hear. You have many, many examples and strengths from which to draw information to successfully answer questions. Using the three-minute, three-question rule is an invaluable tool. Don't forget to use it.

Evaluation

You gain strength, courage, and confidence by every experience in which you really stop to look fear in the face.

—Eleanor Roosevelt

17

Evaluating your performance

As they say, hindsight is 20/20.

Evaluating your performance after each interview, like hindsight, will help you improve future interviewing opportunities. To help you evaluate your performance after an interview, use the following questions as a guideline. Each question prompts you to judge different aspects of your interview. After the questions, you will find the interview self-evaluation form; use it to calculate your evaluation results. You can print the self-evaluation form from my website at **www.csn4jobs.com.**

Dress:

1. Was my dress professional and appropriate for the interview?

2. Was I dressed at the level of the interviewer?

3. Was I over-dressed for the occasion?

4. Was I comfortable with what I wore?

Preparation:

1. Did I have an understanding of the job going into the interview?

2. Did I have a better understanding of the job after the interview?

3. Did I know enough about the job?

4. Did I know enough about the hiring manager/interviewer?

5. Did I know enough about the company?

6. Was I able to use my pre-interview research to positively assist my interview?

7. Did I have good/appropriate questions to ask the interviewer?

8. Did I get business cards from each person with whom I interviewed?

9. Did I have a resume to give the employer, as well as other information he/she asked for (i.e., references, portfolio examples)?

Body language:

1. Was I aware of non-verbal clues before and during the interview?

2. Did I make a good first impression?

3. Did the interviewer seem interested in what I had to say?

4. Did I convey interest during the interview with my body language?

5. Did I fidget too much or appear too nervous?

6. Did I practice effective relaxation techniques?

Responses:

1. Was I comfortable with my responses?

2. Was I prepared to answer the questions the interviewer asked?

3. Did I answer the questions in a reasonable amount of time? (too short, yes and no answers, or too long, more than two minute answers)

4. Did I use effective examples to answer the majority of the questions?

5. Did I qualify and quantify my answers?

6. Was I able to effectively convey my skills and talents as they related to the job requirements?

7. Did I use the three-minute, three-question rule?

Closure:

1. Did I ask for the job?

2. Were all of my questions answered?

3. Did I ask the interviewer when they would make a decision and when I should expect to hear something about their decision?

4. Did I thank the interviewer(s)?

5. Did I send a thank you letter(s) within 24 hours?

After you have answered these questions, take a minute to evaluate what you did satisfactorily and what needs improvement. This process done after each interview will assist you in improving during each consecutive interview.

Below is a self-evaluation form; use it immediately after each interview. Assess your performance; ask yourself what worked and what needs improvement. You may print this form from my website at **www.csn4jobs.com.**

INTERVIEW
SELF-EVALUATION

Dress:

Preparation:

Body Language:

Responses:

Closure:

Well Done

Needs Improvement

Note: All forms are available on my website at **www.csn4jobs.com**

18
Follow-up

When the interview is over it's time to begin working on the follow-up. Make sure you have the names (or business cards, if possible) of all the individuals with whom you interviewed.

You may want to add the receptionist to your thank you list. Thanking a receptionist for her/his help will do more good than you can imagine. I know of companies that chose not to extend an offer of employment to a top candidate because of rudeness to the company receptionist. I have also seen a receptionist go to bat for an average candidate because they were friendly and respectful.

In fact recently I was having a hard time getting to the vice president of a prospect company so I called her administrative assistant. We chatted briefly and she asked me how I thought she could make more money but not leave her current position. We discussed some ideas that I had that seemed helpful. Before we ended our conversation, she thanked me for the advice and told me she would personally see to it that the VP got back to me. She did. By noon the next day I had a return call from the vice president!

Just a note of caution. Be sincere with the secretaries and receptionists. They're usually the most savvy people at the company!!!

Methods of follow-up

Thank you letters are the most common form of follow-up. Do not forget to write them. Write and mail them within 24 hours. There are three types of thank you letters.

1. Hand-written, intimate

2. Computer-written, formal

3. Creatively-written, industry specific

Most employers don't care which type of thank you note you send. However, they usually do care whether or not you send one. A good rule of thumb is that the more formal the work environment for a particular job, the more formal the thank you note. If the job is creatively oriented—for example a graphic designer—you may want to submit a creative thank you. On the other hand, if you're applying for a job as the senior bookkeeper you'll probably want to stick with a formal note. Aside from general guidelines, you may want to consider the following:

1. How well did you get along with the interviewer? Did you connect with him/her? How personal was your interview?

2. Is the position creatively or analytically oriented?

3. Was the interviewer dressed professionally or casually?

4. Did you gather personal/professional information that bears repeating?

5. Is there an interesting twist regarding your interview that would remind the hiring manager who you are?

6. Is there something interesting that would relate to the industry and remain within the bounds of professionalism that would be appropriate? For example, I once sent a clever thank you note to the hir-

ing manager for a major pharmaceutical company. On the front of the note was a Native American medicine man. The hiring manager loved it!

Other considerations to keep in mind when choosing the type of thank you letter to send is how much time you have before the hiring manager chooses a final candidate. With this in mind, you should consider the following:

1. Will mailing your letter take too long?

2. Would emailing or faxing your letter be more effective?

3. Hand delivering your letter.

4. If in doubt, maybe the gatekeeper or department secretary can make suggestions that would work. (Note: make sure you have their name before you call back to get information from them).

Writing a thank you letter

The intent and content of your thank you letter should be similar to your cover letter in that in reiterates your reasons for writing. Reprise your skills and accomplishments as they relate to the position, your interest in the job and working for their company, and include your contact information for follow-up. As with the cover letter, avoid the canned form letters, but be brief and to the point. I do think it is important to cover the basics while making your thank you personally relevant and not too generic. Below I have outlined a simple four-paragraph thank you letter as a guideline.

Sample Thank You Letter

June 27, 2001

XYZ COMPANY (Use all uppercase letters for the company name)
Attention: Ms. Jane Smith
Re: Executive Administrative Assistant to the President
123 East Company Street
Anytown, Arizona 12345

Dear Ms. Smith:

Thank you for taking the time to interview me for the position of Secretary/ Receptionist last Wednesday, June 27.

I would like to reiterate how interested I am in working for The XYZ Company. Your company sounds like a perfect fit for me because you offer an enthusiastic atmosphere that encourages creativity and fosters professional growth as it maintains aggressive industry standards.

Further, I believe that my skills and qualifications closely parallel those you outlined during the interview. In particular, I think that my strong customer service background would greatly benefit the XYZ Company as will my ability to effectively organize and prioritize my work activities. I am also experienced at assisting the executives to whom I report in staying on top of their priorities and supporting them with my excellent written and verbal communication skills. I feel I would be a tremendous asset to your department. Not only am I confident that I could do the job well, I am also certain that I would work well with the team members in your department.

Again, thank you for your time and consideration. I would like to follow up during the next week to confirm my status for the wonderful opportunity. In the meantime, if you have any questions please contact me at your convenience at 123-456-7890.

Sincerely,

Andrea C. Wood
Voice: 123-456-7890
Email: **acwood@email.com**

When you have completed your thank you note, read it aloud to hear how it sounds. Make sure it flows smoothly, that the grammar is perfect, and that you have details and names spelled correctly.

Sending the creative thank you letter

The professional and intimate thank you letters are similar. However the creative thank you letter is another matter. When you send a thank you letter, you need to be certain that it is appropriate for your audience. Sending the wrong type of thank you might end in disaster.

For example, several years ago when I was doing outside sales in the employment industry I had a client that I really wanted to impress. After my meeting I sent a clever thank you that I believe helped to land the account.

After my presentation I hand delivered a mug with our company logo on it, filled with all brown, chocolate covered candies and one red chocolate covered candy placed on top. The note I attached read: "Thank you for considering us as your source for top quality employees. We really do deliver top candidates backed by one-of-a-kind service." To this day, that client remembers that candy!

I cannot imagine anyone not appreciating receiving candy as a thank you, but there are instances where sending something unusual will not work. If sending a creative thank you is appropriate, it can make a huge difference. Consider it carefully.

In closing, remember to send thank you letters within 24 hours of your interview. Make them neat and easy to read and free of grammatical and/or spelling errors.

The follow-up telephone call

This is another option to consider carefully. Not every hiring manager will appreciate your call. However, many expect some type of follow up to indicate just how interested you are. I tell people the more the job your applying for relies on your follow up with people, the more an employer will most likely want you to phone them after an interview. In fact, 56 percent believe follow up is necessary and 85 percent of those employers are impressed with follow up attempts. Only 25 percent of employers say you absolutely must follow up, and 12 percent say don't call at all.

For instance, I have a good friend who is a district sales manager for a reputable pharmaceutical company. She hates to have people call her after she interviews them. She tells them if she's interested, she'll call them. If they attempt to call her after the first interview, she often disqualifies them from the running stating that if they can't follow simple directions that they'll make big mistakes later.

On the other hand, I have a business associate who manages the IT division for a national healthcare insurance information distributor who won't consider a candidate unless they attempt a follow up call with him. He is hard to get to and he likes to see how persistent a potential employee can be. His philosophy is if someone wants to work for him, they should prove it.

So how do you know what to do? Ask! When you ask the interviewer if it is okay to follow up with them pay attention to their body language and non-verbal behavior. If they want you to call back, and they are seriously interested in you as a potential finalist, they will be candid. On the other hand, if they appear vague and explain that they will call you, don't plan to call them. In this case, you may want to follow up with the secretary and ask for his/her help. As a third party in the interviewing process, the secretary can often provide more information in a less awkward way about your rank in the selection process.

19

Other after-the-interview things to do

Companies may wish to follow up with you for other reasons. If they are seriously pursuing you as a potential candidate for employment, you will most likely have some type of pre-employment testing to do.

Pre-employment testing

Companies often use pre-employment testing to determine hiring eligibility. If you get to this point in the hiring process, you are probably being considered seriously for employment. Some tests or questions may be unintentionally biased. Refer to chapter 11 regarding illegal questions before pre-employment testing.

Perhaps the most common and most expected is the **drug/alcohol test**. Sixty-seven percent of the nation's largest companies test their employees or applicants for drugs, according to a 2001 survey by the American Management Association, a New York based consulting firm. You can expect anything from a questionnaire to blood, urine, or hair analysis testing. If turned down due to failing these particular tests, here are some considerations:

- Ask the company if they performed a validation test (a double-check of your test).

- Are you taking prescription or over-the-counter drugs that may have interfered with the test? If so, make sure the employer knows before the test.

Another type of testing you may encounter after your initial interview is **psychological testing**. Do not try to outwit the test. Honesty is always the best policy here! These tests may include personality and career interest tests.

Clerical and administrative positions often require **skills testing.** You should expect keyboard, mathematics, spelling and dexterity testing. Besides clerical jobs other jobs where skills testing is done include occupations in assembly, technical-oriented areas and accounting, or telephone skills testing for customer service personnel. If you use a skill that is "measurable" on the job, expect some sort of test to prove your expertise. You may not be tested but if you are prepared you stand a much better chance for success.

Employers may give you questionnaires that test your **honesty and dependability.** Surprisingly, most companies do not check references. However, you should always expect to have references checked.

A note of caution here. As I mentioned earlier it's a good idea to have a friend or colleague check your references to see how they check out. Never provide a personal or professional reference before you first determine if that reference will respond positively. Though it is illegal to divulge negative or potentially harmful information about a candidate, you would be shocked by how many people get negative references from sources that they thought were going to be helpful.

Some companies have **assessment centers**. Various exercises simulate day-to-day (usually management) activities that include teamwork, conflict management, decision-making, as well as oral or written communication skills. Expect companies to ask you to perform a job duty as part of the interviewing process. For example, you may be asked to make a PowerPoint™ presentation as part of the interviewing process if the job for which you are applying requires you to make presentations using PowerPoint. Make sure you can do what you say you can do!

Priority testing is simply a way for an employer to see how you might prioritize the normal activities of a day on the job with a few emergencies thrown in for good measure. Consider the goals of the company and the objectives of the job. Look at all of the activities first before making any choices. If in doubt, you can always ask yourself what will help you attain your most significant goals, and what could you delegate and what could wait until later.

Usually this type of test will come after you have interviewed. If you have taken notes and listened, you will have a thorough understanding of the goals and main concerns regarding the position, which will help you make the best choices for prioritizing.

The best advise for testing is to stay as cool and calm as possible. Keep in mind that this is not the only job. It may feel like the only job, or you may need the job desperately; but keep your cool. Be yourself and try to relax. It will be your best chance for success.

What to do when you *DON'T* get an offer

It is only a job! Realize too, that it is not the only job. Not getting what you want is sometimes a fantastic stroke of good luck.

I have a friend who was passed up for what seemed an exceptional opportunity with a dot com company. The salary was significantly higher than what he had been earning—almost double in fact. He came in as their runner-up and understandably felt devastated. However, when the company filed chapter 11 and eventually went out of business six months later he was thankful for his good fortune.

The flip side is another candidate I worked with who did take a lucrative position with a company that went belly up shortly after her hire, which put her back on the job hunting circuit.

Dot coms aside, after an unsuccessful interview you may want to consider contacting the interviewer to give you feedback regarding the selection process and why you did not make the final selection. Don't expect them to tell you why they did not select you. Most hiring managers are very uncomfortable with this. But it's worth a try. If they do provide you with answers, thank them and take the advice to heart.

What to do when you *DO* get an offer

When you've gone through the interviewing process and are fairly certain you're going to get an employment offer, you have two questions to consider. First, whether the new position is right for you; and if so, what sort of offer you are willing to accept (chapter 21 offers a thorough examination of evaluating the offer).

To begin evaluating an offer consider the following questions:

1. Does the new position meet the criteria defined before the interviewing process?

2. Will the new job improve your level of personal and professional satisfaction?

Compensation is usually the key determining factor in your decision whether or not to accept a position. There are other factors to consider—for example specific elements of the job that include management responsibilities, challenging or interesting job duties, ability to do the job, and how well you get along with management, peers, and immediate superiors. Other elements to consider are work environment, required travel, location and size of the company as well as advancement and earning potential.

There are so many issues facing you in determining a potential offer, yet it's surprising how many people don't evaluate and compare their current position with their potential opportunities. In the following chapter, I will discuss in detail how to completely evaluate an offer once it's on the table.

Regardless of where your priorities lie in deciding to accept or decline an offer, it's best to compare the facts of your current position and potential opportunity.

20

Offer and salary negotiations

I'd like to do a quick review of the salary negotiations we discussed in chapter 13. As I've stated before in this book, good information often bears repeating.

Basic salary negotiation formulas

There are two formulas by which to negotiate your salary. You need to decide before you start the negotiation process which method you are most comfortable using.

The simple salary negotiation formula

First, you may choose traditional negotiating where the company offers a salary and you counter offer until you reach an amount with which both parties are comfortable. If you choose this method, you will want to use the Salary Negotiating Formula. As you can see, this salary negotiating formula is simple.

Ask for the difference between what the company is offering and what you want. When both sides compromise towards the middle you usually get what you want and the company feels they get a break in the final offer as well. For example:

Company offer: $57,000   You want: $60,000   Ask for: $63,000

The difference between $57,000 and $60,000 is $3,000. You add the difference which is $3,000 to what you want which gives you

$63,000. Keep in mind that most companies offer you less than what they are willing or able to offer. They expect you to counter offer.

A note of caution here: if the salary formula places the asking salary in an unreasonable range, you will need to compromise. If in doubt what to ask for, always opt for something reasonable and fair. The Internet (try **www.salary.com***) is a good resource for checking salary standards for specific jobs.*

The bottom-line-walk-away method

This is not a "maybe" or an "about" question. This is what your actual bottom line is. The term bottom line refers to the amount of compensation you feel is absolutely necessary to accept the job offer. If, for example, you really want $62,000 but would consider $60,000 and would settle for $57,000, then you have established your bottom line. Your bottom line of $57,000 is the absolute bottom amount you would accept or walk away from if the offer came in one dollar less.

You determine your bottom line. If the company offers you more than your bottom line, accept the offer. If, on the other hand they do not offer you what you want, reveal to them your bottom line and let them "up the salary" or walk away.

New perks and unusual deals

Most career opportunity offers come together quite easily with little or no need for haggling. Sometimes, though, it takes a bit of creativity to satisfy both parties.

Salary can pose problems if what you want is higher than the originally published amount, or if it compromises other salaries within a department. For example, if your salary requirement exceeds that of someone with whom you will be peer in a department you can imagine the stir it might cause if word of your higher salary leaked. I believe that it is unprofessional to discuss salary or income with co-workers. Some companies have policies that forbid it, and for those that do the above scenario could prove disastrous.

Often companies find ways to satisfy your needs and their inter-departmental issues at the same time. There are ways to compensate you adequately with means other than your annual salary. Here is a list of added perks that you can ask for to boost your earnings and earning potential without upsetting the equilibrium within a department.

1. A **sign-on bonus** to be paid in cash on your date of start

2. A **discretionary bonus** to be paid in a lump sum, or over a period of time

3. A generous **relocation bonus plan** to be paid on your date of acceptance to cover expenses but which can be used at your discretion

4. A **performance bonus** to be paid after 30, 60, or 90 days, assuming you meet or exceed pre-determined goals and objectives

5. An **accelerated review** which would occur sooner than average, usually after three to six months of employment, in which you would receive a salary increase

6. An **early participation** or **stock options** in the company's bonus, stock purchase, or pension plan, or other employee benefit program

Look for these types of perks from companies that need to be creative when pursuing potential candidates. Smart candidates know that overall compensation consists of more than salary alone.

21
Evaluating an offer

If everything about the new job opportunity looks satisfactory, accept the offer. If you're expecting an offer from a second company, you should let the second company know about your offer right away, so they can speed up their decision, if needed. That way you won't jeopardize two potential offers!

Once an offer is on the table, it should be accepted or refused within a few days. There are some circumstances which allow more time to make a decision. If the offer is reasonable and what you expected plan to respond within a few days. If on the other hand you have legitimate concerns, or you have unanswered questions, now is the time to contact the company and bring them up. Rather than telling the employer you'll think things over, you may want to consider using the following: "Mr. Hiring Manager, this jobs looks very good to me and I am very interested in coming to work for your company. First, I have a few points I'd like to clarify before I give you a definite start date."

Once the questions are answered to your satisfaction (or not), you should accept the offer by the next business day, if possible. If you choose to decline the offer, remember once you decline you have very little hope of going backward and reopening an offer for employment. Make sure you're certain you want to make a career move before you make a final decision to accept an offer.

At the end of this chapter are four evaluation forms, which you may print from my website at **www.csn4jobs.com**. These forms allow you to compare an offer to your current position, the community to which you may relocate and a benefits checklist. The **opportunity comparison** form allows you to check those attributes that each position offers. You simply total the checks in each column; the column with the highest number offers the most potential. You will also want to consider each attribute's individual importance to you as you make your final decision.

The second evaluation form, the **opportunity compensation comparison** allows you to compare total compensation packages between your current position and the new company's offer. Pull out your calculator and tally the totals from each column. The column that offers the highest total is the better compensation plan. As you know, salary is not always the most important factor in determining job satisfaction.

The third evaluation **benefits to family comparison** form focuses on how your career move might affect you and your family. The **benefits checklist** is a simple checklist to compare how the benefits packages between companies measure up.

Upon completion of your evaluation, look at the total picture. If you are still uneasy about an offer, it probably isn't the right job. Learn to trust your instincts. When a job is right, it feels right. If you're not excited about a company and an offer they've presented, something is wrong. Your level of enthusiasm is usually a good indicator of a worthy opportunity or a not so good career move.

Note: Learn to trust your instincts. When it's right, it feels right!

There are an amazing number of benefits to consider and compare when looking at a potential opportunity. Carefully weigh all of your options and closely measure what is important to you.

Look at what employers across the nation offer their employees. According to an article in the Gannett News Service titled *Work—life quality benefits increase* (based on a report from research performed by Hewitt Associates, a Management Consulting firm), companies are offering new benefits and perks to attract and keep the best employees.

The 1999 Hewitt Associates study surveyed 1,020 employers and found:

1. About 57 percent of employers provide flextime

2. 47 percent offer part-time employment

3. Approximately 28 percent offer telecommuting

4. 20 percent offer compressed work schedules

5. Summer hours are available for 12 percent of American workers

6. Overall, 90 percent offer some type of child-care benefit

7. 47 percent of companies offer eldercare, which is up 7 percent from 1997

8. Almost 31 percent offer adoption assistance with an average maximum reimbursement of $3,100

9. 52 percent of employers provide some type of on-site convenience or personal services such as

    - ATM (34 percent)

    - Banking services (22 percent)

    - Travel services (18 percent)

    - Dry cleaning services (15 percent)

    - Discount purchase services (12 percent).

10. 60 percent of employers surveyed offer casual dress or business casual dress to employees

11. 12 percent of the employers offer a 12–week unpaid leave required by the Family and Medical Leave Act of 1993

12. 75 percent provide employees with educational assistance, and personal and professional growth assistance

As you can see, American employers are opening their eyes—and their arms and pocketbooks—to the special needs and wishes of the American worker. The above mentioned benefits are just some of the special perks that you may have an opportunity to obtain through your offer negotiation. If your offer is solid and you're confident, you may wish to ask for or about the above benefits. Most company representatives will outline these benefits if they are available before an offer. It's okay to ask. Just be careful not to go overboard with what you ask for. You don't want to start a great new job and have the label of being greedy before you even begin.

Generally, the higher the level of demand for your particular expertise the more lucrative the benefits will be. Recently I read that the newest, most unique benefit for high tech "need to haves" is to be able to bring their pets to work! I'm not kidding. I even know of several companies that offer pet insurance. I'll never cease to be amazed at what the American employer will do for top talent!

Directions: Compare the position you have now with the one you are considering, using the following factors.

Opportunity comparison

Current job	New opportunity	Job factor under consideration
		Position title
		Your fit with the corporate culture
		Rapport with management
		Rapport with co-workers
		Working environment
		Management responsibilities and advancement opportunities
		Project management responsibilities and advancement opportunities
		Decision-making autonomy
		Freedom to effect change, or capability to make a difference
		Promotion potential
		Challenging and appealing work
		Base salary
		Benefits (see benefits check list)
		Ability to effectively perform job duties
		Industry stability and growth cycle expectations
		Future salary advancement and earning potential
		Desired location
		Travel requirements
		Miscellaneous considerations or value-added perks
Total:	Total:	

Score: _____ **Current job**

_____ **New opportunity**

_____ **Opportunity differential (+/-)**

Directions: Compare the job you have now with the one for which you are applying, to evaluate the following factors.

Opportunity Compensation Comparison

Current job	New opportunity	Factor to consider
$	$	Base salary
$	$	Management bonuses (perks)
$	$	Value of stock
$	$	Profit sharing
$	$	Pension
$	$	Retirement/401K (or similar)
$	$	Tax savings accounts
$	$	Reimbursement of expenses
$	$	Expense account
$	$	Relocation expenses
$	$	Insurance for self
$	$	Insurance for family/dependents
$	$	Insurance for auto/vehicle
$	$	Property taxes
$	$	State taxes
$	$	Other taxes
$	$	Other additional expenses
$	$	**Totals**

Score: _____ Current job

_____ New opportunity

_____ Opportunity differential (+/-)

Directions: If you need to compare the community you now live in and the community of the new opportunity where you may relocate, evaluate the following factors:

Benefits to family comparison

Current community	New community	Factor to consider
		Size of community
		Climate, average high/average low
		Cost of living differential (from above)
		Schools
		Churches, synagogues, temples etc.
		Special attractions
		Special features
		Proximity to extended family
		Entertainment opportunities in community

Score: _____ **Current community**

   _____ **New community**

   _____ **Community comparison differential (+/-)**

Directions: Compare the job benefits you have now with the benefits of the company for which you are applying.

Benefits checklist

Current employer	New opportunity employer	Benefit to check, evaluate and consider	Yes, benefit offered	No, benefit not offered
		Medical coverage (PPO, HMO, other)		
		Chiropractic coverage		
		Holistic/alternative Healthcare coverage Dental coverage		
		Vision coverage		
		Short-term disability		
		Long-term disability		
		Life insurance		
		Executive life insurance		
		Flex spending tax-free account for daycare		
		Flex spending tax-free account for medical		
		Stock purchase		
		Stock options		
		Flextime scheduling		
		Telecommuting		
		Vacation		
		Personal leave		
		Medical (maternity/family) leave to 12 weeks Sick leave		
		Professional sabbatical		
		Senior dependent care (nursing home)		
		Miscellaneous, not listed		

Score: _____ Current employer benefits

_____ New opportunity employer benefits

_____ Community comparison differential (+/-)

22

Have I told you to prepare?

You're now equipped to handle the interviewing process like a pro. You're armed with a plan that will work if you work the plan. If you follow the simple guidelines in this book, you can greatly increase your chances for success during the interview process. The secret, really, is being prepared.

Just a few more words...

I have a few more words of wisdom. As you might guess, before beginning work on this book, I spent a considerable amount of time interviewing many business colleagues and associates for their opinions on interviewing. I felt like I needed the input of industry professionals to make this book complete and valuable.

Of the many hiring managers and business professionals to whom I spoke, some had interesting things to say about the hiring process and interviewing. For example, one manager I talked to said, "If the applicant perks up when talking about their job accomplishments and knowledge it is an excellent sign of a person who enjoys their job."

Another employer, a good friend of mine who is responsible for an impressively successful sales district for one of the country's largest pharmaceutical companies, told me she looks for people who instinctively "know" how to act. She says they, "call me by name, reach for my hand, look me straight in the eye. I notice if they are at ease, lack-

184 > Help! I Need A Job

ing confidence, or if they are just anxious, but confident." She continues, "I look for someone who listens with their eyes and ears."

While other managers look for attention to detail, good attitude, and strong work history without large employment gaps, others are focusing on traits like genuine personalities, honesty, and professional appearance. The range of what is top on the list for hiring managers is varied, but there remains a constant thread in each of their appraisals: excellence. Excellence in character, excellence in application, or excellence in general—whatever is the goal of the hiring manager—one thing stands true: employers are looking for the best of the best.

When you make the choice to be the best, and it is a choice, you must plan for success! For those who map their success there must be a plan, a strategy and a game plan.

I have talked about four fundamentals in this book: prepare, practice, observe and evaluate. Those fundamentals, like the traits of successful people, run parallel. To achieve true excellence one must prepare a plan for success and practice vigorously to attain one's goals.

Furthermore, a triumphant careerist must pay careful attention to what is happening in the world. They must ask what is happening, what's changing and how should they best respond to it all. Finally, those in the league of the best evaluate their performance and their career track. They update and make changes in order to keep ahead of the game.

Therefore, whether you're interviewing or planning for a successful and satisfying career—prepare, practice, observe and evaluate. Map your career, and plan for your success.

I call it CareerMapping™.

In closing, I would like to add that career success could begin with your map to the top. My life's motto has always been, "If you do the right thing, you can do anything." So in choosing your career pathway, do the right thing: that thing which is right for you, that choice that when you make it takes you to excellence.

Best wishes for a successful interview!
Katreena Hayes-Wood

About the Author

Katreena Hayes-Wood is a speaker, facilitator, author and executive search recruiter. She has spent the past 17 years helping others with their careers. She has delivered seminars and workshops to students and adults on career development and career discovery. Topics include "How to interview for a job," "How to re-engineer your career™," and "Trends in employability."

Since starting her own company Career Services Network in 1997, Katreena has helped hundreds of professionals obtain satisfying careers. She currently specializes in competitive market information research. She also co-founded Strive for Students, a camp that helps high schools students discover and build satisfying and successful careers.

Formerly associate director of career services for a national private college, Katreena works with school districts, parents, and government agencies assisting them in establishing strong career development programs. She also volunteers with schools providing programs about career information and job-search skills for students.

She is past President of the Arrowhead Millennium chapter of American Business Women's Association (2000–2001) which she co-founded in Glendale, Arizona, and was elected their woman-of-the-year in 2000.

For more information about Katreena Hayes-Wood or her upcoming books and seminar schedule, write to her at 7942 West Bell Road, Suite #C5-422, Glendale, Arizona 85308, or call (623) 561-6838, or you may visit her website at **www.csn4jobs.com.**

Appendix

Quick Reference

Action verbs to use on your resume.

Advertising	Communications	Creativity	Management
Accounted for	Approved	Arranged	Administered
Convinced	Counseled	Conceived	Attained
Generated	Demonstrated	Created	Conducted
Improved	Disseminated	Designed	Contracted
Influenced	Edited	Developed	Controlled
Launched	Facilitated	Devised	Coordinated
Marketed	Instructed	Enabled	Directed
Persuaded	Interviewed	Enhanced	Enacted
Promoted	Moderated	Formulated	Established
Recommended	Participated	Innovated	Exceeded
Represented	Presented	Invented	Executed
Secured	Presided	Originated	Expanded
Sold	Served as	Packaged	Headed
	Wrote	Refined	Implemented
		Reshaped	Incorporated
		Resolved	Initiated
		Solved	Instituted
		Structured	Maintained
			Managed
			Masterminded
			Obtained
			Organized
			Performed
			Produced
			Reduced

			Repositioned
			Retained
			Revised
			Strengthened
			Supervised
			Trimmed
			Undertook

Negotiations	Research	Resourcefulness	Technical
Assured	Automated	Accomplished	Analyzed
Closed	Classified	Awarded	Arranged
Determined	Determined	Corrected	Budgeted
Evaluated	Developed	Diverted	Catalogued
Investigated	Differentiated	Eliminated	Compared
Mediated	Equated	Identified	Compiled
Negotiated	Experimented	Improved	Completed
Proposed	Investigated	Pioneered	Computed
Sorted	Related	Rectified	Decreased
	Searched	Solved	Distributed
	Solved	Strengthened	Enlarged
	Synthesized	Surpassed	Examined
	Theorized		Expanded
			Generated
			Improvised
			Increased
			Indexed
			Leveraged
			Redesigned
			Reengineered
			Reorganized
			Restructured
			Reviewed
			Revised
			Scheduled
			Single-handedly...
			Synthesized
			Systematized
			Verified

Quix Fix

Take a couple of minutes and read over the Interviewing dos and don'ts. Many of the listed hints will be familiar. Some you have undoubtedly heard already, maybe even more times than you care to, but as with all good information it often bears repeating.

Interviewing dos

1. Be prepared!

2. Send interview appointment confirmation cards (email or mail depending on amount of time until your interview)

3. Be prompt, and arrive at least 10 minutes early

4. Listen attentively and take notes

5. Express ideas clearly

6. Use strong examples from work history to demonstrate your match for the job

7. Be brief and to the point (keep answers to two minutes or less)

8. Act confident, as well as enthusiastic

9. Pay attention to body language

10. Answer question with examples

11. Relate positive experiences

12. Ask appropriate questions (prepare some in advance; see chapter 9 and 10)

13. Stress your qualifications

14. Be factual

15. Think before you speak

16. Smile and make appropriate eye contact

17. Give a firm handshake

18. Always, always send thank you notes within 24 hours

19. Dress professionally and appropriately (see chapter 4)

20. Have extra copies of your resume (resumes, see chapter 7)

21. Have your business card resume (See chapter 3)

22. Have your cheat sheet ready (see chapter 14)

23. Ask for the job!

Interviewing don'ts

1. Fail to prepare!

2. Talk too much (take two minutes or less to answer any one question)

3. Answer yes or no—elaborate your answers appropriately

4. Talk about politics, religion, personalities, or controversial topics

5. Name drop

6. Say you can do anything

7. Argue

8. Criticize the interviewer

9. Complain or gossip about your current or past employer(s), supervisor(s), or co-workers

10. Talk about personal problems, relationships, or family

11. Wear "funky" too-loud fashions (see chapter 2 on appropriate dress)

12. Bring up salary (interviewer should mention salary first)

13. Smoke or drink alcohol during a luncheon interview

14. Forget to ask for the job!

Following these simple rules will greatly increase your chances of success during the interviewing process.

Quix Chex

If your interview is in fact tomorrow, use this Quix Chex list to make sure you have everything you need in preparing for your interview.

The interviewing checklist: things you should do, be, or have

- Detailed job description of job for which you are interviewing

- Information on company, including address and phone number

- Information about the person with whom you will interview

- Receptionist's name at that company

- Professional resume (see chapter 7)

- Cheat sheet (see chapter 14)

- Business card resume (see chapter 3)

- Portfolio with notebook and pen for taking notes at the interview

- Professionally dressed (light on top, dark on bottom; see chapter 4)

- Professionally groomed (simple accessories, nothing extreme; see chapter 4)

- A great attitude and smile, good eye-contact, firm handshake

- Ask for the interviewer's business card before you leave

- *ASK FOR THE JOB!*

Try to have everything laid out the night before.

When organizing the night before an interview, go over the above list and make sure everything is ready to go. Have your directions on a sticky note along with your portfolio notebook. I recommend you keep a small, zipper bag, (clear works best so you can see what's inside), in your vehicle with some basics like breath mints, sticky notes, aspirin, clear fingernail polish (for those nasty pantyhose snags/runs), fingernail clippers/scissors, five dollars (for unexpected parking expenses), and a small mirror (just in case you have broccoli in your teeth).

You will also want to keep your portfolio notebook loaded with a resumes, a pad of paper for notes, a pen and pencil, business cards (if possible, or reasonable), your quick reference phone number book, a city map and your all-important cheat sheet (with extra 3"x5" cards for new and improved versions).

I hope you're not laughing! I'm serious about the zip bag in your car and your loaded portfolio, because there is nothing more frustrating than planning to arrive on time and to be running late for an appointment because you can't find something important you need to take to your interview.

Here it comes…prepare, prepare, prepare!

References

Additional resources and suggested Reading

For a more compressive and up-to-date resource list go to **www.csn4jobs.com**.

Resources:

Helpful Internet search engines

www.google.com
www.askjeeves.com
www.about.com
www.yahoo.com
www.excite.com
www.dogpile.com

Helpful websites for job search and/or resume posting:

www.csn4jobs.com
www.monster.com
www.headhunter.com
www.careerbuilder.com
www.dice.com
www.ajb.dni.us
www.jobweb.com
www.myjobsearch.com
www.job-hunt.org
www.nationjob.com
www.job-search-engine.com

jobstar.org
www.hotjobs.com
careers.yahoo.com
www.jobbankusa.com
www.flipdog.com

Jobs with the federal government:

www.fedworld.gov/jobs/jobsearch.html
www.hrsjobs.com/
www.dol.gov

Helpful websites for relocation:

www.relocationcentral.com
www.homefair.com
www.monstermoving.com
www.erc.org
www.relojournal.com
www.relocationexpert.com
www.relolinks.com
123relocation.com
www.insiders.com/relocation

Helpful websites for cost-of-living indexes:

nt.mortgage101.com/partner-scripts/1150.
asp?p=buyerstrust
www.coli.org
www.datamasters.com

Helpful websites for U.S. salary standards:

www.salary.com
www.rileyguide.com/salguides.html

Suggested Reading:

Adams Press. *City Job Banks.* Holbrook, Mass. Adams Media Corp. 2000 (they offer specific city job banks for larger metropolitan areas).

Adams Press. *Internet Job Search Almanac.* Holbrook, Mass. Adams Media Corp. 2000

Bowles, Richard N. *What color is your parachute?* Berkeley, Calif.: Ten Speed Press, 2000

Braham, Barbara J. *Finding Your Purpose.* Menlo Park, Calif. Crisp Publication, Inc. 1991

U.S. Department of Labor, *Occupational Outlook Handbook, 2000–2001 Edition.* Chicago, Illinois, NTC/Contemporary Publishing Group, 2000

0-595-22075-4

www.ingramcontent.com/pod-product-compliance
Lightning Source LLC
Chambersburg PA
CBHW030929180526
45163CB00002B/506